UNDERSTANDING

GENERATION-SKIPPING

TRUSTS

INTRODUCING THE
SEQUOIA TRUST™

CHUCK BANKER

2006 Edition

UNDERSTANDING GENERATION-SKIPPING TRUSTS
Copyright 2006 by Charles D. Banker. All rights reserved.

This publication is designed to provide accurate and authoritative information in regard to the subject matter covered. It is sold with the understanding that the Author is not engaged in rendering professional services. If professional advice or other expert assistance is required, the services of a competent professional person should be sought.

ISBN 0-9777218-0-9

Printed in the United States of America.

10 9 8 7 6 5 4 3 2 1

ACKNOWLEDGMENTS

First and foremost, I want to thank my family - - the Banker girls - - my wife, Maria, and my daughters, Jaclyn, Alyssa, and Kerry for their love, support, and ability to deal with my undying intensity and passion to be the best, a lesson that I trust and hope that they carry on for their lifetimes.

Second, I have to thank my great friend and terrific attorney, David Pratt, for his consistent excellence and his input in crafting this book.

Third, Jack and Cay Lee! Great friends, brilliant people! Jack, thanks for your editing and editing and . . . Cay, for providing me with the perfect name for the Trust that will last for many lifetimes - - the Sequoia Trust™!

Fourth, Andy Bucklee, a guy who suddenly became my boss after ten years of friendship, and never changed! Andy's support has been extremely meaningful to me, and my entire family will be grateful for years to come.

Finally, to my friends and family, you know who you are. I am a lucky guy to have your love and support - - the greatest gift any person possibly could ask for!

And, of course, dedicated to Audie, my mom, simply the best! I can't believe it's been eleven years, and it still feels like yesterday . . .

CONTENTS

IMPORTANT INFORMATION

There are complex legal and tax implications associated with the various strategies illustrated, and you must consult with your own tax and/or legal advisors to determine whether or not any plan or program illustrated is appropriate for you. Any tax statements contained herein were not intended or written to be used, and cannot be used for the purpose of avoiding federal, state or local taxes.

Effective planning requires that you consult with your attorney. The Author and his representatives are not authorized to practice law or to provide legal or tax advice. The material contained in any illustration is not a substitute for consultation with a competent legal advisor and should only be relied upon in conjunction with his or her advice.

Furthermore, the results indicated by any of these strategies are dependent upon our understanding of current federal and state income, gift and estate tax laws as presently interpreted by the Internal Revenue Service and state tax authorities. Any change in such tax laws or interpretations could affect the result illustrated.

In particular, under the Economic Growth and Tax Relief Reconciliation Act of 2001 ("EGTRRA"), the Federal estate and generation-skipping transfer taxes are currently scheduled to be repealed for taxable years ending (and in the case of the generation-skipping transfer (GST) tax, generation-skipping transfers occurring) after December 31, 2009. However, for gifts made, decedents dying, and generation-skipping transfers occurring after 2010, the law, as in effect immediately prior to EGTRRA, will be re-enacted. Changes in these provisions may affect the appropriateness and efficacy of the techniques illustrated.

The results shown in any analysis are neither guarantees nor projections, and the interest rate assumptions, rates of return, tax rates, and other costs are for illustrative purposes only. The result of this analysis may differ significantly depending on the facts assumed in the analysis.

The illustrations contained herein are hypothetical in nature, for discussion purposes only, and do not reflect an actual product offered by an insurance company or approved for sale in any state or jurisdiction. While the illustrations are intended to generally reflect a possible insurance solution, the utilization of actual insurance products may produce values more or less than those shown. You should consult actual illustrations for details, assumptions, and disclosures regarding those premiums and those values which are contractually guaranteed in the policy. The policies illustrated may require yearly insurance premiums, and the payment of such premiums may have gift tax consequences.

P R E F A C E

This book is about the ultimate estate plan, the gift of financial security to your children and their descendants through effective estate planning. It will show how to structure a plan that will benefit your family for generations to come.

A critical part of a successful plan is to minimize or eliminate estate, inheritance, or other taxes that may be due upon your death. This book will focus on federal transfer taxes. If you do the requisite planning with help from a competent professional, your family will thank you for your hard work in accumulating assets and for your foresight for setting in motion an action plan to preserve and use these assets.

So now that you have managed to accumulate sufficient assets for retirement and feel that there might be a bit left over to ultimately pass to your children, how do you keep the tax collector out of your pocket?

Many people believe that it's just not possible to reduce their federal estate tax liability. This is not true. You can put in place an estate plan that minimizes the amount your family must pay in taxes upon your death and/or the death of your spouse. Not only is this possible, it is relatively simple, provided you acquire the appropriate advice from a qualified professional to help implement the best plan for you!

This book focuses on generation-skipping planning, a complex topic in the estate tax laws. The name, "generation-skipping," creates two common misconceptions that tend to immediately cause a lack of interest. First, many people, as well as some professional advisors, believe that Generation-Skipping Trusts are too complicated and are only useful to the ultra-wealthy. Second, many people think that Generation-Skipping Trusts are established to transfer assets to grandchildren, rather than children. This could not be further from the truth.

Once you have read this book, the facts and ideas presented should make you want to call your estate planning professional immediately.

Generation-skipping planning is about leaving your assets to your children and, after their lifetimes, to future generations of your family. It does not refer to skipping your children, it's about skipping the payment of estate taxes, possibly for hundreds of years. If structured properly, your children's inheritance can also be protected from ex-spouses and creditors!

Your goal should be to create a plan that will allow your children and future generations of your family to have control and access, but to insure that the assets are protected from estate tax, divorce claims, lawsuits, and bankruptcy. I strongly recommend generation-skipping planning to those who have managed to accumulate wealth that they wish to transfer to their families, whether they have a couple hundred thousand dollars or a couple hundred million dollars.

Until now, there has not been a good single resource available to explain the merits of generation-skipping planning in an easy to understand format. With this book you have a relatively simple guide that explains why generation-skipping planning is beneficial for anybody wishing to provide his or her family with the ultimate gift - - financial security.

Assuming you wish to utilize a generation-skipping planning strategy, the first step is to hire the right attorney and take an active role in helping him or her craft what will become the foundation of your family's wealth for generations to come. This involves a variety of tax and non-tax matters, and requires a lot of thought.

Introducing the Sequoia Trust™

In order to assist you with this task, I decided to work with my attorney, David Pratt, to develop our own version of a Generation-Skipping Trust that might be used as a guideline to assist in the development of the most suitable trust based on your particular goals and objectives. I refer to this as the "Sequoia Trust™."

The reasons why I selected this name can be summarized as follows:

- the Sequoia tree lasts for thousands of years in spite of the influences of man and nature, in many ways similar to a trust that continues for centuries or longer, despite the enumerated risks;

- the Sequoia tree dwarfs all other trees found in forests, as this trust does in relation to other types of trusts;

- the Sequoia tree develops roots and branches, analogous to the family that continues to grow over time but remains bonded together; and

- the Sequoia tree is only found in the United States, the land where every person has the freedom to use the tax laws to your best advantage.

The Sequoia Trust™ can be crafted in many ways, depending on the choices that you make regarding the many issues discussed in this book - - the ongoing operation of the Trust, the amount of access available to trust beneficiaries, the desired level of flexibility provided to trustees and/or beneficiaries, and the underlying investments.

A sample of the Sequoia Trust™ is available to assist you and your attorney with the crafting of the most appropriate Trust for you and your family.

Please contact the author at www.chuckbanker.com for additional information.

INTRODUCTION

Many of us are of the opinion that the tax laws are written by the wealthy to favor the wealthy. In other words, those with the ability to obtain the best advice have an advantage that may not be available to the general population.

At times, it seems that a disproportionate level of wealth has remained in the hands of certain families in this country. Their last names are easily recognized and are synonymous with wealth. The question is, what have these families done to successfully retain and protect their wealth? The real answer is not what they have done, but what their ancestors did years ago to establish a long-term plan to avoid estate taxes and creditors, thereby sustaining their family's wealth for generations.

BACKGROUND

At one time, it was possible to completely avoid estate taxes by establishing a trust that provided the following generation with what was referred to as a "life estate," or the right to enjoy the trust assets without taking legal possession. In essence, rather than leaving assets directly to their children upon death, wealthy families instead created trusts for their children and their descendants that provided them with the ability to access trust funds for their living expenses.

There was no limit to the amount that could be transferred into these Trusts, so most wealthy families were able to simply leave their assets to these Trusts and eliminate all estate tax liabilities upon a beneficiary's death. Because the trust beneficiaries did not own the trust assets, there were no assets that were subject to estate taxes upon their deaths. Similarly, if the beneficiary became involved in a divorce or a lawsuit, or filed for bankruptcy, the trust assets were not subject to any claims due to this lack of legal ownership.

The net result was that these families were able to amass great fortunes that would remain in their bloodlines, protected from estate taxes and third parties for as long as the property remained in Trust. Most of these Trusts were designed to last as long as possible based on the laws in effect when the Trusts were created.

In 1976, Congress curtailed this practice by creating a tax on generation-skipping transfers. The generation-skipping transfer ("GST") tax was substantially amended in 1986, and remains in effect today.

The rationale behind the GST tax is that families should pay estate tax at the end of every generation. If wealthy families are allowed to leave their assets to a Generation-Skipping Trust that postpones estate taxes by one or several generations, the government loses an opportunity to impose estate taxes. The GST tax is designed to limit, not eliminate, these transfers.

GENERATION-SKIPPING PLANNING AND YOU

Most of us are focused on setting aside enough assets to retire comfortably, as we should be. Life is about setting priorities, the most important of which is your own financial well-being. No one should consider giving up control of or access to their assets unless they are emotionally and financially prepared to do so.

In any event, whether you have sufficient assets for retirement and are seeking to establish a plan to transfer wealth to your family at your death, or if you are fortunate enough to have more than you need for daily living and wish to transfer assets to your family during your lifetime, proper planning is in order. The first step is to find an experienced and qualified tax attorney who is well-versed in estate and gift tax planning. The next step is to become educated so that you have a better understanding of your options.

As in other parts of your life, once you have an understanding of your various options, you need to determine which alternative makes the most sense for you. This decision-making process involves the following three inter-related questions:

- Does the proposed strategy offer tax advantages?

- Is the strategy appealing from an investment standpoint?

- Are you emotionally comfortable with the strategy?

Your legal, investment and tax advisors can assist you with the first two decisions, which should be based on fact. However, the most important issue is whether a proposed strategy makes sense from an emotional perspective.

This is an issue that can only be answered by you, not by any advisor. Let's discuss each of these questions to give you an idea of what Generation-Skipping planning is all about.

TAX ADVANTAGES

Rather than leaving assets directly to family members, your assets can be placed in a trust that can be controlled by the family members and that can be accessible to them. You, as grantor or creator of the Generation-Skipping Trust, are entitled to limit their control and access if desired, or you can provide them with liberal rights of control and access.

Although your family members may be entitled to control and/or use these assets during their lifetimes, if the Trust is properly structured, they are not considered to be the owner for legal or tax purposes. From an estate tax standpoint, this is a major advantage.

The amount any individual may transfer at death without incurring any federal estate tax is currently $2 million. In addition, any individual may transfer $2 million at death free of any GST tax.

Under current law, the federal estate tax exemption and the GST tax exemption are scheduled to increase to $3.5 million in 2009. There is no federal estate tax or GST tax in 2010, but in 2011, the federal estate tax and GST tax will be reinstated to the tax structure of 2001. At that time, each individual will have an estate tax exemption of $1 million and a GST tax exemption of $1 million (indexed for inflation). It is widely believed, however, that Congress will set a higher permanent exemption level than that which was in place in 2001.

You can choose to allocate your estate tax exemption or GST tax exemption to a Trust for your descendants. If you do so, the property held in the Trust will never be subject to estate or GST tax as long as the Trust remains in effect and no further additions are made to the Trust. Your family member who is the beneficiary of the Trust is not treated as the owner of the assets in the Trust, so he or she will not pay estate or GST taxes upon death.

As a matter of fact, even if Congress decides to change the estate tax laws in future years, assets housed inside the Generation-Skipping Trust would in all likelihood remain exempt from estate and GST taxes. Accordingly, the objective is to make the transfer sooner rather than later, make the Trust as large as possible, and extend the duration of the Trust far into the future. Each of these issues is discussed later in this book.

THE INVESTMENT ASPECT

If there were no estate tax system, wealthy families would obviously continue to prosper even more rapidly than the current system allows. The actual impact of estate taxes over an extended period of time may surprise you.

EXAMPLE 1

COMPOUNDED IMPACT OF ESTATE TAXES

Let's assume that a married couple transfers $4 million (the maximum amount that can be transferred to a Generation-Skipping Trust in 2006 without being subject to a GST tax) to a Trust that grows by 6% annually during the next 120 years. In the first instance, the assets pass to a Generation-Skipping Trust that avoids estate taxes during the duration of the Trust, whereas in the second instance, 45% of the assets are paid to the IRS every 30 years in estate taxes:

YEAR	GST PLANNING	NO GST PLANNING
1	$ 4,000,000	$ 4,000,000
30	$ 22,973,965	$ 12,635,681
60	$ 131,950,763	$ 39,915,107
90	$ 757,858,045	$ 126,088,636
120	$ 4,352,750,992	$ 398,303,932

While both strategies provide generously, the long-term benefit of generation-skipping planning becomes apparent throughout the term of the Trust. Which column would you select, assuming you had the opportunity?

THE EMOTIONAL PERSPECTIVE

The use of Generation-Skipping planning also makes sense from an emotional perspective. While removing the assets from the risk of being depleted by estate taxes is adequate reason in and of itself, there are additional considerations that are perhaps more important than the tax advantages. Divorce rates are at an all-time high, and the risk of leaving assets to former sons- or daughters-in-law is a major concern for many parents. The use of a properly drafted Generation-Skipping Trust can effectively minimize this risk, increasing the likelihood that your assets will ultimately benefit your children and future generations of your family.

Protection from creditors is also of paramount importance. For instance, the problem of increasing medical malpractice suits has forced doctors and other medical professionals to take action to protect their assets from potential litigation. By transferring assets into a Generation-Skipping Trust rather than as an outright bequest, the risk of a creditor pursuing these assets is substantially reduced.

The same benefits, protection from creditors, apply well beyond the scope of employment-related risks. When a family member is involved in litigation, has a judgment against him or her, incurs medical expenses beyond his or her means, or is forced into bankruptcy, the assets inside the Generation-Skipping Trust can be protected from these claims.

Frankly, the battle to accumulate wealth involves overcoming the efforts of the various "creditors and predators" waiting to pounce, namely, the tax collector, ex-spouses and in-laws, and those bringing lawsuits. The transfer of assets to your children without them being exposed to estate taxes, divorce claims and lawsuits is an opportunity that should not be missed.

FAMILY PERSPECTIVES

Too frequently, when generation-skipping planning is being considered, the topic of "ruling from the grave" becomes an issue. There are some people who are accustomed to being in control of their assets, and wish to extend their control beyond their lifetime. The Generation-Skipping Trust makes perfect sense for these people, because they can create whatever rules and restrictions they desire. However, others may find the specter of "ruling from the grave" distasteful.

Therefore, it is important to study the benefits of generation-skipping planning from the perspective of the beneficiary. First, if properly-structured, these trusts can effectively provide the beneficiary with very liberal rights to control and enjoy the trust assets. Second, the assets remain available to the beneficiary irrespective of any divorce or creditor concerns. Third, the assets remain exempt from estate and GST taxes. When viewed together, this equates to the gift of financial security, the ultimate objective of an effective estate plan.

There is a risk, however, of insulting your sons-in-law and daughters-in-law, as they typically do not have any rights to the Trust assets. Frankly, these assets are specifically designed to remain in the bloodlines of the person who first created the Trust. Of course, if desired, the Trust can be structured to provide access to an in-law in the event they were to outlive their spouse who is a beneficiary of the trust.

Another issue focuses on the treatment of step-children. Again, the person who creates the Trust has the privilege of creating as restrictive or liberal a trust as he or she feels is suitable. Typically, however, the enjoyment of Trust assets is limited to lineal descendants, which do not include step-children, but does include those who are legally adopted.

IMPORTANT PLANNING CONSIDERATIONS

While many parents are excited by the prospect of providing their children with the gift of financial security, they worry about spoiling them or removing all incentive to become independent and successful. Others are concerned about the ability of their children to handle wealth, or wish to limit the amounts that become available to them. There are a variety of restrictions that can be included to address these issues, which will be discussed in Chapter Three.

By now, you should ask yourself the question, "Why would I not want to use a Generation-Skipping Trust given the choices?" It is obvious that, for many, a properly-executed Generation-Skipping Trust is a powerful estate planning and wealth preservation tool, and should be used by more people than currently take advantage of this technique.

As you continue reading, you will learn about the various rules and restrictions relating to the GST tax so that you will have the necessary information to help you work with your tax attorney to create your own version of the Generation-Skipping Trust.

CHAPTER 2

THE RULES & REGULATIONS

Without being overly technical, this chapter provides you with a background of the provisions of the Internal Revenue Code that impose a tax on generation-skipping transfers. I will attempt to simplify this law, and discuss the most common applications, based on 2006 tax laws.

SYNOPSIS OF THE LAW

The GST tax is a flat tax imposed, in addition to any gift taxes or estate taxes that may apply, on assets transferred to a "skip person" - - a person who is two or more generations younger than the person making the transfer. The tax also applies to transfers in trust that benefit a "skip person." For example, a transfer of assets from a grandparent to a grandchild, either directly or via a trust, is subject to the GST tax.

It is important to understand that every person has an exemption, currently $2 million, which allows them to make a certain amount of generation-skipping transfers free of any GST tax. The GST tax rate is equal to the highest federal estate tax in effect in the year of the transfer, and is applied in addition to estate taxes.

In 2006, the GST tax is 46%. Assuming a person in the highest estate tax bracket makes a transfer in excess of their exemption, they could face the loss of more than 63% of the amount transferred!

EXAMPLE 2

CALCULATION OF TRANSFER TAXES

Assume Mr. Smythe, who has already used his GST tax exemption, makes a bequest of $1 million upon his death to each of his four grandchildren with the provision that the resulting estate and GST taxes are to be borne by the property. The $4 million transferred to his grandchildren would be subject to estate taxes of 46%, a total of $1,840,000. In addition, the net amount passing to the grandchildren - - $1,479,452 - - is subject to the GST tax at the same 46% rate, resulting in an additional tax of $680,548.

Accordingly, of the $4 million transferred to the grandchildren, a total of $2,520,548, or 63%, would pass to the IRS, leaving $1,479,452 to be divided among the four grandchildren.

This makes it crystal clear that those who desire to transfer assets to grandchildren or other "skip persons" run the risk of leaving the lion's share of their assets to the IRS unless they have the appropriate plan in place. Fortunately, with creative planning, a person can take advantage of his or her exemption and leave substantial amounts to future generations without incurring such taxes, thereby creating the foundation of his or her family's net worth for generations to come.

THE EXEMPTION

As stated above, every person has the opportunity to make a genera-tion-skipping transfer that will avoid the GST tax, but the Internal Revenue Code places a limitation on this amount. Under current law, this limitation, or "exemption," is identical to the amount that can pass free of estate taxes.

The applicable exemption and GST tax rates are as follows:

YEAR	EXEMPTION	TAX RATE
2006	$2,000,000	46%
2007/8	$2,000,000	45%
2009	$3,500,000	45%
2010	NO FEDERAL ESTATE TAX	

Beginning in 2011, when the amount that can pass free of estate taxes is scheduled to revert to $1 million, the GST tax exemption is also scheduled to revert to $1 million, adjusted for inflation, and the GST tax rate would be calculated at 55%, which will be the highest estate tax rate in 2011. However, most tax advisors believe that the above schedule will be amended well before 2010.

You need to be very careful in your planning to avoid the disaster of losing 63% or more to the IRS as a result of uninformed or negligent planning!

TYPES OF GENERATION-SKIPPING TRANSFERS

The GST tax exemption applies when assets are transferred to a person who is two or more generations younger than the donor. Typically, this refers to a grandchild or great-grandchild, whether the children are natural or adopted. Where transfers do not involve bloodline relationships, a person who is between $12^{1/2}$ and $37^{1/2}$ years younger than the transferor is considered to be one generation younger, and a person who is more than $37^{1/2}$ years younger is considered two generations younger for purposes of this tax.

Each time a generation-skipping transfer is made, a timely allocation of the generation-skipping exemption should be made in order to avoid the imposition of the GST tax. While in some cases the Internal Revenue Code may automatically allocate the exemption, in most cases it is better to allocate the exemption on a Federal Gift (and Generation-Skipping Transfer) Tax Return (Form 709). When the value of the property transferred exceeds the lifetime exemption, the GST tax applies. This occurs at several points in time, depending on the type of transfer.

The GST tax only applies when assets are actually transferred to the "skip person." There are three different types of transfers:

DIRECT SKIPS, which are outright transfers to a person two generations younger than the person transferring the property that occur during lifetime or at death. For instance, a direct skip occurs when a person makes an outright gift, names a skip person as the beneficiary of an IRA, annuity or life insurance policy, or leaves them assets pursuant to a will or living trust.

TAXABLE TERMINATIONS, which typically refer to transfers in trust for the benefit of multiple generations, occur when the interest for the benefit of the older generation who is not a skip person is terminated by reason of death, lapse of time, or otherwise. Thus, if a person transfers property to a trust that pays income to children for their lifetimes after which the assets are to divided among the grandchildren, a taxable termination occurs upon the death of the last surviving child and the assets are distributed to the grandchildren.

TAXABLE DISTRIBUTIONS occur when there is a distribution from a trust to a skip person, other than a direct skip or a taxable termination. An example of a taxable distribution would be when a trust that pays income to children and/or grandchildren actually makes a distribution to a grandchild.

There are certain transfers that are excluded from GST taxes, including transfers made directly to grandchildren that qualify for the annual $12,000 gift tax exclusion, payments for educational or medical costs, and transfers in trust that qualify for the annual $12,000 exclusion, provided the transfer is solely for the benefit of, and includible in the taxable estate of, such grandchild. Thus, transfers that are made in trust for the benefit of multiple beneficiaries are not exempted, and are subject to the GST tax.

CALCULATION OF GST TAX

The amount of the transfer that is subject to the GST tax is calculated differently depending on the type of transfer that takes place. As stated above, each person's GST tax exemption may be allocated to any generation-skipping transfers at the time of transfer. This is a relatively simple matter with respect to outright transfers, or direct skips occurring at death as the excess transfer over the available lifetime exemption is subject to the GST tax.

However, the calculation becomes more complex if distributions are made in trust, or where lifetime transfers have been made, or where multiple transfers occur, thus requiring an allocation of the lifetime exemption. In this case, the amount that escapes the GST tax is based on how and when the transferor's generation-skipping exemption is allocated. A few examples will help you understand this concept.

EXAMPLE 3
OUTRIGHT TRANSFERS

In 2006, Mr. Smythe passes away, leaving a total of $3 million to his three grandchildren. This is a direct skip, and is subject to the GST tax to the extent the transfers exceed his lifetime exemption. Mr. Smythe allocates his $2 million lifetime exemption to the direct skips of $3 million, leaving $1 million subject to the GST tax. A GST tax of 46%, or $460,000, is assessed in addition to estate taxes.

EXAMPLE 4
ALLOCATION OF GST EXEMPTION

In 2006, Mr. Smythe creates a trust that provides income to his daughter for her lifetime, and upon her death, the trust assets are to be distributed to his three grandchildren. Because the trust is a Generation-Skipping Trust, a tax will typically apply at the time of any taxable distribution from the trust (i.e., a distribution to a grandchild), or upon the taxable termination of the trust at the daughter's death.

Importantly, the Generation-Skipping Trust is funded with a total of $1 million, and $1 million of Mr. Smythe's generation-skipping exemption is allocated to the transfer. Because 100% of the trust's value was subject to the GST exemption, and assuming no additional contributions were made to the trust, all future distributions from this Trust will escape the GST tax, even if the Trust assets at the time of distribution are worth well in excess of the maximums. In addition, Mr. Smythe still has $1 million of his exemption remaining to be used at a later date.

EXAMPLE 5
PRO RATA ALLOCATION OF GST EXEMPTION

In 2006, Mr. Smythe passes away, leaving $2 million directly to his children, and establishes a Generation-Skipping Trust with another $4 million. Again, a GST tax would be due at the time of any taxable distribution to the grandchildren, or upon the taxable termination of the trust. In this case, Mr. Smythe would have allocated his entire $2 million generation-skipping exemption to the Generation-Skipping Trust.

Because the Trust had a value of $4 million at the time it was funded, 50% of the Trust value will escape GST tax (the $2 million allocated exemption, divided by the total transfer of $4 million). Thus, every time a trust distribution is made to a grandchild or younger generation, 50% of such amount is subject to a GST tax as a taxable distribution. If the trust is terminated, or upon the death of the last surviving child, 50% of the value of amounts paid from the trust to a grandchild or younger generation would be subject to the GST tax as a taxable termination.

In these situations, a better practice is to divide the Trust into one trust wholly exempt from the GST tax and one wholly non-exempt to the tax. Distributions to the children should be made from the non-exempt trust and distributions to grandchildren and more remote descendants should be made from the exempt trust.

CHAPTER 3

CRAFTING THE TRUST

Now that the concept of generation-skipping transfers is understood and deemed to be desirable for your estate plan, the next step is to hire an experienced and qualified tax attorney to craft a document that will become the foundation and centerpiece of your family's wealth for generations to come. It is vitally important that your attorney truly understands how Generation-Skipping Trusts can be constructed for your family's benefit.

In considering your choice of a qualified tax attorney, remember that you get what you pay for. Simple mistakes made by an inexperienced attorney can literally cost your family a fortune. Generation-skipping tax laws are very complex and require careful drafting by a person who is experienced at this specific task.

In order to find a competent attorney, begin by speaking with other professionals who may be aware of a person who possesses the required expertise. You can consult the Martindale-Hubbell directory at your local library or at 'www.martindalehubbell.com' on the internet. This will provide you with a listing of local attorneys and a description of their particular backgrounds.

Another excellent resource is the ACTEC listing, which refers to the American College of Trust and Estate Tax Counsel, which is a group of highly-experienced estate tax attorneys throughout the United States. Their website is 'www.actec.org'. If the state where you reside certifies attorneys in specific areas of the tax law, your attorney should be board-certified in Taxation and/or Wills, Trusts and Estates.

The next step is to be involved in the process with your attorney to craft a document that fits your particular set of objectives. The document will necessarily include all of the appropriate tax language, but it is important for your personal desires to be reflected in the ongoing operation of the Trust. Remember, this Trust will continue for many years to come and you are the person who has the responsibility of creating whatever rules and restrictions you feel are appropriate!

SEPARATE SHARES vs. A SINGLE TRUST

Ordinarily, it is preferable to divide the trust into separate shares for each beneficiary so that family harmony is maintained. This would avoid the risk of children fighting over access to a single trust, but may create problems with later born grandchildren.

Most long-term trusts are established on a "per stirpes" basis. This is a relatively simple concept that specifies that each branch of a deceased person's family receives an equal share of the estate, regardless of how many people are in that branch.

EXAMPLE 6
PER STIRPES PLANNING

Mr. Smythe has three daughters. When he and Mrs. Smythe pass away, the maximum amount that they can leave free of GST taxes will pass to a trust that will be divided into three equal shares for each of their children. If a child pre-deceases them, her 1/3 share will be divided into equal shares for each of her children, if any. Upon each of the daughter's deaths, her trust will be sub-divided into separate equal shares for her children.

Some people prefer to establish shares based on a "per capita" formula. In this case, the Trust would be divided into shares based on the number of beneficiaries at such time.

EXAMPLE 7
PER CAPITA PLANNING

The "per stirpes" formula described above dictates that, upon the death of any of the three daughters, her 1/3 interest will be split among her respective children. If Mr. and Mrs. Smythe had used a "per capita" formula, the amount that would be split among their grandchildren would be based on the total number of all of the grandchildren so that each grandchild receives an equal amount.

Frankly, this formula is not as common as "per stirpes" as it tends to favor those families that have the most children.

OPERATION OF THE TRUST

The next step is to focus on the trust mechanics. This is where the attorney needs to know your intentions, so stay involved. This requires you to determine those issues of importance to you, and to take an active role in describing them to the attorney.

The most critical issues that need to be addressed in crafting the Trust include control, access, and flexibility. Let's explore each of these issues, and move towards determining the most important features of a Generation-Skipping Trust that is designed to be the foundation for your family's wealth for generations to come.

CONTROL

The control issue is one of the most critical components of the Generation-Skipping Trust. In general, if the trust is designed to provide liberal access to Trust assets, the use of family members as trustees may be the most desirable alternative. As a matter of fact, it is not uncommon to name the primary beneficiary as the sole trustee, or to name a co-trustee, but provide the primary beneficiary with the right to fire any co-trustee and name a replacement.

If the grantor is seeking to be somewhat restrictive, or if the trust beneficiary is incapable of acting as trustee (because he or she is a minor, is disabled, or is financially inexperienced), the use of a professional or corporate trustee might help to assure that the Trust provisions are followed. The combination of a professional or corporate trustee and a family member can also be effective.

It is also possible to allow the primary beneficiary to decide who will become successor trustees for the benefit of the following generation. The issues regarding the selection of trustees are discussed in much greater detail in Chapter Four.

ACCESS

The grantor of a Generation-Skipping Trust has the privilege to decide when and how much of the Trust assets will be distributed to the beneficiaries. For many families, the primary attraction of generation-skipping planning is to effectively provide beneficiaries with control (as trustee) and access (via distributions of trust income plus principal in designated circumstances) without exposing the Trust assets to estate tax, divorce claims and creditor concerns.

However, there are many instances where there exists a need to restrict or limit distributions. These considerations typically involve tax issues, a desire to keep trust beneficiaries productive members of society, or for asset protection considerations.

ESTATE TAX CONSIDERATIONS

From an estate tax perspective, the most important concern in establishing a Generation-Skipping Trust is to make sure that access is not so broad that the family member is considered to legally own the Trust assets for estate tax purposes, thus defeating the purposes of the Trust. Accordingly, there must be some type of limitation regarding access, but this can be crafted so that there is more than adequate financial security.

This is typically handled in one of two ways. First, if the beneficiary is going to serve as the sole trustee, the trust must include an "ascertainable standards" provision that allows a beneficiary to access principal when needed for "health, education, maintenance or support." Second, if you want to provide the beneficiaries with unrestricted rights to access trust principal, a friendly co-trustee could be appointed who would be given the power to distribute income and/or principal for any reason deemed appropriate.

In addition, a Trust can include a special provision known as a "five and five" power. This provides a trust beneficiary with the power to demand the greater of $5,000 or 5% of the trust assets in any given year. For maximum flexibility, the Trust can include both provisions, so that the beneficiary can make distributions to himself or herself for health, education, maintenance, and support; and the co-trustee can make additional distributions for broader purposes.

Importantly, as long as the assets remain inside the Generation-Skipping Trust, they escape estate taxes and remain protected from creditors. Thus, the Trust should not require mandatory distributions, as that could expose the assets to the claims of the beneficiary's creditors. Without mandatory distributions, the Trust can grow free from estate taxes and creditors in the event there is no need for income.

BENEFCIARY INCENTIVES

In crafting the Generation-Skipping Trust, the ability to restrict enjoyment of the assets may be as important as making the Trust adaptable to changing circumstances. In many cases, parents may wish to limit access to Trust assets for a variety of circumstances. For instance, many children simply do not have the ability to manage their financial lives responsibly. Others may have certain personal conditions (e.g., mental or physical disability, past drug or alcohol use) that would make restrictions desirable. In other situations, parents may be concerned about creating "trust fund babies" who have no incentive to earn a living in light of their access to the Trust assets.

The key is deciding how much access makes the most sense. While this may be a subjective matter regarding your children when the Trust is first established, when you consider that the Generation-Skipping Trust could last hundreds of years, the issue becomes much more important.

Of course, the person who creates the Trust can create whatever rules he or she feels are appropriate. This could conceivably include limiting access to a specified percentage of the Trust rather than all of the Trust assets. One could also link distributions to specific goals, such as completing college, or to encourage certain types of behavior such as remaining employed, or participating in charitable endeavors. Similarly, it is not uncommon for a Generation-Skipping Trust to have restrictive provisions to deny access or to terminate distributions in the event of failure to graduate, or criminal activity, or failing a drug test.

ASSET PROTECTION MATTERS

For many families, the opportunity to provide for their children while protecting the assets from their lack of ability or judgment to handle assets, or from ex-spouses and/or creditors is more important than the tax benefits. This is typically solved by using what is known as a "spendthrift provision."

A spendthrift provision prohibits a trust beneficiary from transferring his or her interest, whether voluntarily or involuntarily. This prevents a child from selling his or her interest in the trust or from using it as collateral for a loan. In addition, it prevents a creditor from accessing a child's trust interest directly, meaning that a beneficiary could not be forced to take a distribution or sell their interest in the trust to satisfy a creditor's claim.

In essence, this means that a creditor will have to wait until a distribution is actually made before it can pursue such amounts.

Of course, no trust distributions will occur until all matters are settled, thereby protecting the assets for future trust beneficiaries.

FLEXIBILITY

One of the key considerations with a Generation-Skipping Trust is that it is anticipated to last for an extended period of time. Consequently, it should have the ability to adapt to changes in the family dynamics as well as the tax laws. Many of these provisions are discussed below.

AMENDING THE TRUST

Remember, this Trust is expected to last for several generations, perhaps hundreds of years. While every effort can be made to create a flexible trust that will stand the test of time, unfortunately we cannot see into the future. In all likelihood, there will be changes in family circumstances or tax laws that warrant changes in trust provisions. However, great care must be taken in including such a provision, as improper drafting can cause adverse gift or estate tax consequences.

One of the most appealing changes in trust planning of the past several years has been the use of what is known as a "trust protector provision" that establishes a process whereby the terms of the trust can be amended. Typically, this involves the appointment of an independent person, or a committee, who retains the privilege to make such changes when necessary.

ABILITY TO CHANGE TRUSTEES

The ability to effectively control the Trust assets while obtaining the benefits of estate tax protection and freedom from divorce and creditor concerns is the most important feature of the Generation-

Skipping Trust. By providing the beneficiary or another person with the authority to remove and replace the trustee in certain circumstances, the ability to control the Trust assets is dramatically enhanced.

SUPPLEMENTAL DISTRIBUTIONS

If a trustee other than the beneficiary is to make distributions, the trust should provide standards governing the discretionary distributions of trust assets. This ability may be open-ended, or may be limited to specific situations, such as the purchase of a first home, investment in a business or enrollment in graduate school.

DISCRETION TO LEND ASSETS

A popular provision provides the trustee with the ability to lend trust assets to a beneficiary or other person. Typically, an "arm's-length" interest rate must be charged in order to prevent negative income tax consequences. This means that favorable below market interest rates cannot be granted on loaned assets. The ability to lend assets may be open-ended or limited to specific situations, such as the purchase of a home.

RIGHT TO PURCHASE ASSETS FROM GRANTOR

It is common for a Generation-Skipping Trust to be crafted so that the trustee has the right to purchase assets from the grantor if it is in the best interest of the Trust. This provides the grantor with an opportunity to transfer an illiquid asset or a rapidly-appreciating asset to the Trust in exchange for cash. However, if the Trust is not structured with "grantor trust" provisions, lifetime asset purchases could have negative income tax consequences.

The most common use of this provision occurs at the death of the grantor when asset sales may take place without any adverse income tax consequences. This allows a family to preserve the value of the Generation-Skipping Trust, and creates the necessary cash to pay estate taxes into the grantor's estate.

PERMISSIBLE TRUST INVESTMENTS

The Trust should be drafted so that the assets can be used to purchase any type of investment property that has the opportunity for appreciation, including stocks, bonds, hedge funds, and real estate, to name a few. In addition, the trustee should be authorized to purchase life insurance on the lives of the grantor(s) and any trust beneficiaries. This can be particularly appealing as a means of leveraging the ultimate value of the Trust on an income-tax free basis. Again, the Trust must be designed to avoid adverse estate tax consequences.

The grantor should also consider providing the Trustee with the ability to purchase non-traditional assets, including a residence, jewelry, artwork or collectibles. Remember, if the Trust makes a distribution to a beneficiary for the purchase of a home or other investment, the trust distribution passes into the beneficiary's estate for tax purposes, and becomes exposed to divorce claims and creditors. These concerns can be simply avoided by having the trust directly purchase the house or other investment as a trust asset, providing the beneficiary with the right to enjoy the particular asset without exposing it to the above risks.

TRANSFERRING TRUST TO DIFFERENT STATES

We can rest assured that there will be changes in federal and state tax laws in future years. In the event it becomes more desirable to change the situs of a trust to a different state, a mechanism should be in place to accomplish this.

ABILITY TO TERMINATE TRUST

Depending on the level of wealth, it is possible that the value of the trusts will be diluted as the trust is split among more and more people in the family tree. In such cases, it may become too expensive to administer the Trust. In addition, there may be other circumstances where it would be in the best interest of the beneficiaries to liquidate the trust. Again, a mechanism should be included giving the trustee the right to liquidate the trust is such circumstances.

LIMITED POWERS OF APPOINTMENT

Because nobody knows the future, the person who establishes the Trust might want to create the appropriate rules and restrictions that will apply to their children, but allow their children to have a say in the terms of any trusts for their grandchildren. This can be accomplished by using what is known as a Limited, or Special, Power of Appointment, which effectively adds a level of flexibility to an irrevocable trust.

In its simplest form, a Limited Power of Appointment is the privilege during life, or at death, to transfer assets to any person other than yourself, your creditors, your estate or the creditors of your estate. As stated above, this makes the trust much more flexible, and allows a beneficiary to adapt the trust to changes in personal, legal or family circumstances. This is a critical component of a trust that is designed to last for generations.

The power can be broad or narrow, as the case may be. For example, a broad Limited Power of Appointment could be exercised in favor of any individual or entity, including a trust, other than the power holder, the power holder's estate, the power holder's creditors, or the creditors of the power holder's estate. An example of a narrow limited power of appointment is one that could be exercised in favor of your descendants only.

In effect, the use of a Limited Power of Appointment in a Generation-Skipping Trust provides a person with the ability to reconfigure the terms of the Trust or the distribution of the assets among family members, or to charity, if so desired. For instance, if personal or family circumstances warrant, a person with this power can eliminate distributions to a potential trust beneficiary, or leave an increased share of assets to one child over another. Also, the power holder may have the right to make direct distributions to beneficiaries, effectively terminating the trust if they so desire.

CHAPTER 4

TRUSTEE SELECTION

One of the most critical decisions regarding the Generation-Skipping Trust is to select the appropriate person or entity to manage and administer the assets. Before considering who should be named as trustee, the grantor should focus on the responsibilities of the trustee, who is charged with the ongoing operations of the trust and making sure that the actions are consistent with the terms of the trust.

Trusteeship requires many responsibilities, including:

• the exercise of reasonable care in making investment and management decisions consistent with the objectives and terms of the Trust;

• maintaining detailed records regarding the administration of the Trust and account to the beneficiaries of the Trust;

• filing federal and state tax returns;

• fulfilling the duty to diversify trust investments in accordance with the terms of the Trust and state law; and

• maintenance of objectivity, in terms of abiding by the trust document in determining trust distributions.

These are not necessarily black and white issues, and often involve discretion and interpretation of the terms of the trust. The trustee has a fiduciary obligation to the trust beneficiaries to make sure that the terms of the trust are followed with respect to all of these matters.

There are a variety of choices to consider. The trust can name a beneficiary as trustee on their own or in conjunction with others.

A trusted advisor, such as an accountant or attorney, might be considered. Alternatively, a corporate trustee, such as a bank or trust company, can be named.

In many cases, the choice of a trustee depends on whether access is relatively liberal or restricted, and the type of assets that will be owned by the trust. If the trust is designed to provide broad access to the Trust's income, plus principal in the event of need, the grantor may wish to name the beneficiary as trustee. As stated earlier, this is relatively common, provided that the opportunity to access principal is limited to the "ascertainable standards" of health, education, support and maintenance. Again, many attorneys are uncomfortable naming a beneficiary as sole trustee, and will frequently name a co-trustee to make any decisions that involve discretion.

There are many situations where, for one reason or another, a trust is crafted to limit access to trust income and/or principal. Typical examples include trusts for the benefit of a person who is incapable of acting as trustee due to a disability, lack of judgment or inexperience. In these situations it is possible to name another family member or a professional trustee to manage and administer the trust.

As discussed in Chapter Six, however, it is critical that the family harmony be maintained. Thus, the naming of a sibling to make decisions on behalf of another sibling needs to be carefully considered, as such an appointment could potentially cause more disruption than desired.

CORPORATE TRUSTEES

Corporate trustees have not always been the best answer for trust governance. Typical objections to hiring corporate trustees include the expense, the potential for conflict with trust beneficiaries, frequent turnover of personnel, and limited investment menus. However, there has been a revolution in the trust industry that, when combined with careful drafting of the Generation-Skipping Trust, makes the use of corporate trustees, either on their own or in tandem with others, a workable solution in many situations.

There are many advantages of naming a corporate trustee, principally continuity, experience and competence. Unlike an individual, a corporate trustee will be in business for an extended period of time, which is a critical consideration when establishing a trust that is designed to remain in existence for decades if not hundreds of years.

Unlike most individuals, corporate trustees are experienced at carrying out the responsibilities of a trustee - - investment, adminis-tration, and distributions. And, unlike most individuals, corporate trustees are aware of their responsibilities and possess the ability to abide by their fiduciary obligations to the trust beneficiaries. Furthermore, trust companies are held to a higher standard of care than individual trustees.

EXPENSE

Perhaps the primary reason why corporate trustees have been avoid-ed has been based on their traditionally inflexible and expensive fee schedules. While this may have been true in past years and still applies to certain institutions, this is generally no longer the case.

As a matter of fact, as the trust industry has evolved and become more competitive, fee schedules have become the first step in a process of negotiation. Depending on the nature of the desired services, or the extent of related accounts with the trust company, these fees can be substantially reduced, as in any other banking relationship.

In addition, it is unrealistic to compare corporate trustee fees to the absence of such costs if a friendly trustee, such as a family member, or a professional trustee is named. Remember, due to their limited expertise, these people may be required to incur additional costs to handle certain matters such as investment advisory fees, tax return preparation, or legal expenses.

CONFLICT

I have seen too many situations where one family member is given the responsibility, as trustee, to impose limitations on trust distributions to a brother, sister or other relative. There is simply no winner in these matters, and I believe it should be avoided at all costs. In addition, Generation-Skipping Trusts have a natural tendency to result in conflict as the greater the level of distributions to one generation, the lower the value for the succeeding generation.

These are situations that require the use of an uninterested, objective third party, a "referee" to enforce the rules. The referee must possess the required expertise to enforce the responsibilities designated in the trust agreement, and make difficult decisions without emotion. A corporate trustee can fit the bill nicely.

TURNOVER

There has been a great deal of consolidation activity within the trust and banking industry during the past decade, and there is the possibility that this trend will continue. Many families who have avoided naming certain trust institutions for one reason or another have found themselves with that particular institution as a result of a merger or acquisition. Similarly, while current personnel of a trust company may be more than capable, there is obviously no guarantee that they will be around or assigned to any particular trust for an extended period of time.

40

Bank mergers and changing personnel is more than likely going to continue as that is simply the nature of the business world. However, this matter can be addressed relatively easily, assuming the trust agreement is crafted so that the trust beneficiaries have the opportunity to remove and replace a trustee. It is suggested, however, that these provisions require that another corporate trustee must serve in the place of one that has been removed in order to remain consistent with the objectives of the grantor of the trust.

INVESTMENT OPPORTUNITIES

Traditionally, trust companies and banking institutions have been criticized for their conservative approach to investments, and their limited menu of investment options. Again, while this may have been accurate in the past and still applies to certain institutions, this is no longer the case throughout the industry.

As the competition for business within the trust industry has increased, the availability of a broad array of investment options has become more and more commonplace. However, the trust must be properly crafted to provide the corporate trustee with the opportunity to make alternative types of investments.

PROFESSIONAL ADVISORS

Many people who have created trusts have utilized the services of independent and trusted advisors, such as an attorney or accountant, to act as trustee. This approach frequently creates another set of problems and should be carefully reviewed for several reasons.

First and foremost, although an accountant or attorney may be skilled and knowledgeable in his or her particular profession, they typically do not possess the experience or expertise in the role of trustee. Second, in the past, professional trustees were frequently used in order to avoid having to use corporate trustees, who had drawbacks, such as the expense and limitations in investment opportunities. Third, these advisors tend to have a close relationship with the person who created the trust, and could become a source of conflict for younger generations after the person who created the trust has died.

However, retaining professional advisors as a trustee or co-trustee can assist in the ongoing operation of a trust. In this regard, the establishment and use of "Family Offices" has been a welcome trend among many accounting and law firms as a means of sharing the responsibilities of trustees.

INDIVIDUAL TRUSTEES

Most people are inclined to leave their assets directly to their children. This changes when they become better educated about the benefits of generation-skipping planning. They consequently tend to establish trusts that are very liberal, allowing their children to enjoy the use of the trust assets as close as possible to actual legal ownership, but with the additional benefits of protection from estate tax, divorce and lawsuits.

For these people, it makes sense to name the trust beneficiary, typically the child, as his or her own trustee. The concern in these situations, however, is that if the beneficiary is given such broad power to effectively enjoy all trust assets, the IRS (or an ex-spouse or creditor) could ask a court to disregard the trust and all of the benefits associated with generation-skipping planning.

In these cases, it is important to limit access or to name a co-trustee to act in concert with the beneficiary. If a co-trustee is named, the beneficiary is typically given the right to remove and replace such person. In addition, the beneficiary can usually be provided with a power to name future trustees, or to alter the future distribution of trust assets, in the event of a change in family dynamics.

While it might appear to be convenient to name a family member or a friend as trustee from the perspectives of cost and flexibility, the fiduciary obligation, and liability, that go along with being named a trustee must be considered. Obviously, if the value of a Trust erodes due to poor investment performance or a failure to abide by the rules regarding distributions, the entire estate plan will fail.

PRIVATE TRUST COMPANIES

For those families that have substantial wealth, the formation of private trust companies to manage the family's affairs has become more commonplace in recent years. These arrangements provide expertise and continuity via the retention of qualified professionals as employees, and are frequently more personal and less costly than the use of a corporate trustee.

CHAPTER 5

LOCATION OF THE TRUST

Now that you understand what a Generation-Skipping Trust is, you suddenly realize it might make sense for you, whether or not you are wealthy, and whether or not you have grandchildren. Simply put, if there is a way to leave assets to your children where they receive the opportunity to control and access the assets that remain protected from estate taxes, divorce and creditors, why not include this concept in your estate plan?

The selection of the state where the Trust will be established is the next important step. State laws vary concerning the duration, or the period during which the trust will be allowed to remain in existence, the asset protection provisions, and state tax considerations. In most cases, the grantor need not reside in the state where the Generation-Skipping Trust is created, although many of these states do require that all trust administration occur within their state, and/or that all assets be transferred to an account in that state.

A knowledgeable attorney will consider all critical issues - - the permitted duration, the asset protection considerations and tax laws before recommending the jurisdiction that is best suited for the grantor. In addition, the ability to change the location of a trust in light of changing state tax laws is an important provision that offers additional flexibility in a long-term trust.

DURATION OF THE GENERATION-SKIPPING TRUST

When many families study the benefits of generation-skipping planning, they wish to extend the duration as long as possible, possibly forever. Unfortunately, it's not quite that simple.

Each state has its own law that limits the duration of a trust, based on what is known as the "Rule Against Perpetuities." Many states adhere to traditional, or common, law that allows a trust to remain in effect for "the lives in being, plus 21 years." In other words, this restriction allows the trust to remain in effect during the lifetime of all trust beneficiaries alive at the time the trust was created, plus 21 years following their deaths.

EXAMPLE 8

TRADITIONAL RULE AGAINST PERPETUITIES

At the time Mr. Smythe creates a Generation-Skipping Trust, the youngest trust beneficiary is a great-grandchild, age 8. If we further assume that this grandchild lives to age 85, the permitted duration of a Trust based on this traditional Rule Against Perpetuities would be for the lifetime of the great-grandchild from the date the trust was created - - 77 years - - plus 21 years following his death, or 98 years.

In recent years, there has been a trend among many states to enact laws that provide for the maximum duration of a trust as a means of promoting the banking and trust industry within their state. For instance, trusts created in Florida can extend up to 360 years from the date it becomes irrevocable, trusts created in Nevada can extend 365 years, and both Utah and Wyoming have 1,000-year limits.

In 17 other States, plus the District of Columbia, the Rule Against Perpetuities has been abolished, allowing a trust to remain in effect forever. These States are Alaska, Arizona, Colorado, Delaware, Idaho, Illinois, Maine, Maryland, Missouri, Nebraska, New Hampshire, New Jersey, Ohio, Rhode Island, South Dakota, Virginia and Wisconsin.

ASSET PROTECTION CONSIDERATIONS

In addition to having different perspectives regarding the Rule Against Perpetuities, each state has its own view of asset protection. In this regard, certain states have adopted laws that allow for access to trust assets without exposing assets to potential creditors. Caution should be exercised as, in recent years, several states have sanctioned a creditor's ability to access trust assets in situations where the beneficiary had certain privileges that amounted to control, such as the right to change trustees or extend the term of the trust.

STATE TAX CONSIDERATIONS

Of course, in addition to local legislation regarding the duration of trusts and asset protection considerations, the cost of operating a trust must be studied in selecting the location of a trust. In this regard, one of the major costs is state income or intangibles taxes, which vary from state to state.

For instance, two states, Alaska and South Dakota, have no income taxes, and have abolished the Rule Against Perpetuities, allowing a person to create a trust that lasts forever, making these states a particularly desirable location to locate a Generation-Skipping Trust. Several other states, including Delaware and Illinois, do not impose income taxes on local trusts established by nonresidents.

RELATED LEGAL CONSIDERATIONS

There are a variety of other differences in state law to consider when deciding upon the location of a trust. These matters may relate to confidentiality, requirements to notify trust beneficiaries of the performance of trust assets, limitations on trust investments, and/or conflict resolution. In order to ensure that the state's legal requirements are satisfied with respect to the Trust, your tax attorney should consult with a qualified attorney licensed to practice in the jurisdiction where the trust will be administered. In addition, the Trust must have some connection, or nexus, to the state selected, such as the residency of the grantor, beneficiary and/or trustee, the location of trust assets, or the location of trust administration.

CHAPTER 6

FUNDING THE TRUST

Assuming that the concept of generation-skipping planning is appealing and appropriate, another important decision must be made as to whether the Trust should be established during life or at death, or a combination of both. Anyone interested in generation-skipping planning should consider including the appropriate language to capture any remaining GST tax exemption, upon death, in his or her living trust.

TESTAMENTARY FUNDING

A trust created at death is called a testamentary trust. Those who establish a testamentary Generation-Skipping Trust are limited to the exemption in effect at such time. Any excess transfers will result in triggering the GST tax, which is typically undesirable.

Assuming a person dies in 2006 and has not allocated his or her generation-skipping tax exemption during life, he or she can transfer up to $2 million to a testamentary Generation-Skipping Trust, while a married couple can transfer up to $4 million, without creating any potential GST tax.

LIFETIME FUNDING

Those with the means and desire to create a more substantial Trust that will ultimately become the foundation of the family's wealth may wish to engage in lifetime planning. Typically, this includes four different types of transfers:

- giving the annual $12,000 gifting allowances, or $24,000 from a married couple, on behalf of each trust beneficiary;

- giving the $1 million gift tax exemption, which reduces the $2 million estate tax exemption by the $1 million gift, or $2 million on behalf of a married couple;

- lending assets to a trust in expectation that the Trust will be able to out-perform the interest rate charged on the loan, a unique strategy frequently used in connection with the purchase of life insurance; and

- selling interests in Family Limited Partnerships or Limited Liability Companies at a discounted value.

In this chapter, we will explore the more common methods of lifetime funding via annual and/or lifetime gifts. The latter two strategies, which are more complicated, are discussed in greater detail in Chapters Seven and Eight.

ANNUAL GIFT TAX EXCLUSION

Every person is allowed to transfer $12,000 to as many individuals as he or she desires each year free of gift taxes. Married couples have the opportunity to transfer $24,000 annually to any person. For those who have a taxable net worth in excess of the estate tax exemption, it makes sense to make annual gifts to the extent of their comfort level, as every $1 transferred could save at least 46 cents (in 2006) of future estate taxes.

For a gift to qualify for the annual exclusion, all of the following must be true:

- the transfer must be irrevocable, meaning that the person cannot reserve the right to recover the assets in the future;

- the transferor must sever all ties to the transferred assets, meaning that he or she cannot retain any rights with respect to the transferred property; and

- if a transfer is made to a Trust (other than a special trust known as a Section 2503(c) Trust), the beneficiary or beneficiaries of the trust must be given the opportunity to withdraw the transferred asset in order for the gift to qualify for the $12,000 annual exclusion.

LIFETIME GIFT EXEMPTION

In addition to the annual gift tax exclusion, every person has the opportunity to transfer during his or her lifetime the first $1 million of his or her lifetime exemption without any gift tax consequences. Married couples can transfer as much as $2 million during their lifetimes over and above their annual gifts. Those with the means and desire may wish to make gifts to utilize this opportunity sooner, rather than later.

If you have a taxable net worth in excess of the estate tax exemption, for every $1 that your net worth increases, there is an additional 46 cents (in 2006) of estate tax liability. However, to the extent you make annual and/or lifetime contributions, 100% of the income and future growth escapes additional estate taxes.

USING GIFTS TO FUND THE TRUST

If you want to maximize the value of a Generation-Skipping Trust, it is in your best interest to establish and fund the Trust during your lifetime, as all of the future income and appreciation of the Trust assets escapes estate taxes and GST taxes as long as the Trust remains in existence. This concept is illustrated below.

EXAMPLE 9

TRANSFERRING THE LIFETIME EXEMPTION

Mr. and Mrs. Smythe have more than enough assets to cover all of their spending requirements, and are interested in reducing their estate tax exposure. They have been maximizing their annual gift allowances every year, but have not used their $1 million gift tax exemptions.

They subsequently transfer $2 million to a Generation-Skipping Trust that increases to $5 million over their lifetimes. The entire $5 million passes free of estate taxes and GST taxes. If the $2 million had remained in their estate, the entire $5 million would be subject to estate taxes upon the survivor's death.

EXAMPLE 10
LIFE INSURANCE & GENERATION-SKIPPING

Mr. and Mrs. Smythe, a wealthy couple desiring to create a substantial Trust that will provide financial security for their children and, ultimately, future generations of their family, transfer $2 million, using each of their $1 million lifetime gift tax exemptions, to their newly-created Generation-Skipping Trust, and allocate $2 million of their GST tax exemptions to such transfer. The trustee of the trust uses the gifted cash to purchase $10 million of life insurance inside the Trust.

Unfortunately, Mr. and Mrs. Smythe meet an untimely death in 2006. The entire $10 million of insurance proceeds inside the Trust escapes estate taxes and GST taxes since the transfer was part of their generation-skipping exemption. In addition, since the applicable exemption in 2006 is $2 million per person, and Mr. and Mrs. Smythe had only used $1 million of their respective exemptions during their lifetimes, an additional $2 million can be transferred to the Generation-Skipping Trust at such time, assuming their wills or living trusts have the appropriate language to capture their entire exemption.

Based on 2006 tax laws, the Smythe's would have been limited to a total estate and GST tax exemption of $4 million if they had engaged in only testamentary planning, funding the trust at death. However, by using a combination of lifetime planning, leveraging and having updated legal documents, they were able to establish a Trust worth $12 million that would continue to avoid estate taxes and GST tax for generations to come.

52

APPROPRIATE INVESTMENTS

Assuming the trust is drafted broadly, the trustee has the right to purchase a vast array of investment assets, ranging from traditional investments such as stocks and bonds, to life insurance, to real estate, to collectibles. Of course, the long-term investment objective of the Trust is to maximize the value of the Trust at the time it becomes available to the beneficiaries.

INCOME TAX ISSUES

In deciding on what would be the best investment mix, the impact of income taxes must be considered. A Generation-Skipping Trust can be drafted so that any income taxes are charged to and paid by the grantor during his or her life (grantor trusts), the trust itself, or the trust beneficiaries.

GRANTOR TRUSTS

While many people are not particularly enthralled with the prospect of paying income taxes with respect to assets they no longer own, the use of grantor trusts can be an effective way to diminish the value of a person's taxable estate while allowing the Trust to grow as much as possible. In effect, the grantor can make additional tax-free gifts by paying the trust's income taxes.

Grantor trusts can also be used very effectively in connection with a planning technique designed to leverage the value of a Generation-Skipping Trust, commonly referred to as an "Intentionally Defective Trust." This concept is discussed in Chapter Eight.

TRUST TAXATION

If income taxes are to be paid by the Generation-Skipping Trust, careful attention must be paid to the character of the Trust assets. A trust is subject to income taxes the same as an individual. However, the income tax brackets applicable to trusts are severely compressed when compared to the rates in effect for individuals.

For instance, in 2006, a trust reaches the top income tax bracket of 35% after earning only $9,750 of taxable income. Therefore, if the objective is to maximize the value of the Generation-Skipping Trust, the Trust should be funded with assets that have high growth potential, but which generate minimal or no taxable income. This typically includes investments in growth stocks, life insurance, interests in a family business or real estate.

BENEFICIARY TAXATION

To the extent income is distributed to beneficiaries, they will be responsible for the income tax attributable to the distribution. In this event, the character of the income earned by the Trust will pass through to the beneficiaries. For example, to the extent the Trust earns tax-exempt income, distributions to the beneficiaries will also be considered tax-exempt income.

TRADITIONAL INVESTMENTS

Because most Generation-Skipping Trusts are designed with the objective of maximizing their ultimate value, as opposed to providing current income, the use of growth stocks or growth stock mutual funds can be a good choice. As you know, growth stocks offer the opportunity for long-term appreciation and generate minimal amounts of taxable income. If stocks perform to historical standards, they can be a very effective and appropriate investment designed to maximize the Trust value until the time at which income is scheduled to be distributed.

In addition, it makes sense for those providing venture capital or other types of businesses with high growth potential to purchase the stock within the Trust rather than in their own accounts so that the growth occurs free of future tax considerations. Of course, these types of investments should only be undertaken with a full knowledge and understanding of the risks involved, and where appropriate.

LIFE INSURANCE

Many estate planning professionals feel that, under the appropriate circumstances, life insurance can be an excellent funding vehicle for a Generation-Skipping Trust for a variety of reasons, namely:

- unlike stocks, bonds or other investments, life insurance offers tax-free growth;

- typically, Generation-Skipping Trusts are designed to begin making distributions upon the death of the grantor, making life insurance a perfect funding mechanism that provides the highest value at the most appropriate time;

- because certain types of life insurance policies have a guaranteed death benefit, it is an excellent tool that effectively leverages the generation-skipping exemption; and

- the use of life insurance can provide a substantial inheritance, affording the grantor the opportunity to engage in charitable planning activities without diminishing the inheritance to the children.

It is critical, however, to consider the quality of the issuing insurance carrier, as well as the underlying contractual guarantees associated with life insurance. These issues are discussed in Chapter Seven.

FAMILY BUSINESSES

In many cases, the ideal asset to transfer to a Generation-Skipping Trust is a family business, which may consist of stock in a corporation, or an interest in a Family Limited Partnership or Limited Liability Company. Traditionally, it has been very difficult to transfer prosperous family businesses from one generation to the next, primarily due to the combination of estate taxes and a lack of sufficient liquidity to pay such liabilities.

If your family is fortunate enough to own a successful business that you would like to transfer to future generations, the growth is frequently greater than that available with other investments, making it an attractive asset to transfer outside of your taxable estate. By transferring interests in the business to a Generation-Skipping Trust, you can insulate the future appreciation from estate taxes, and thereby protect the ownership of the business for future generations of your family.

There are numerous pitfalls that may arise in the transfer of closely-held business interests, including valuation uncertainty and the possible application of the so-called "Chapter 14" special valuation rules. The assistance of competent legal counsel is necessary in this situation.

REAL ESTATE

For the same reasons that apply to growth stocks, the funding of a Generation-Skipping Trust with real estate can be very attractive. However, if the real estate generates substantial income tax deductions or taxable income, it may not be an appropriate asset. Therefore, this issue must be carefully considered.

COLLECTIBLES

The transfer of collectibles, including art work, precious metals, and jewelry, to a Generation-Skipping Trust can be very effective as a means of passing illiquid assets to family members free of income tax and estate tax. This can be used to avoid the uncomfortable task of dividing assets among children and unintentionally creating a rift amongst your heirs. However, their uncertain value and lack of liquidity and income could make them a less-than-perfect funding vehicle when compared to other alternatives.

CHAPTER 7

LIFE INSURANCE

Once we become educated about the benefits of generation-skipping planning versus outright ownership, the natural inclination might be to transfer all of our assets into these arrangements. However, there are relatively strict limits as to the amount of assets that can be transferred into a Generation-Skipping Trust, and steep taxes will result if these limits are exceeded.

Fortunately, however, those with the means and desire to create more substantial trusts certainly have the ability to do so by utilizing some creative planning techniques. There are a number of ways to accomplish this objective, which are discussed below and in the following chapter. Without question, however, one simple and effective way to expand the value of a Generation-Skipping Trust for future generations is by utilizing a life insurance strategy.

A RE-CAP OF THE FUNDING RULES

As stated earlier, each person is allowed to transfer a limited amount of assets into a Generation-Skipping Trust without becoming subject to additional taxes. In 2006, you are allowed to transfer up to $1 million (or $2 million on behalf of a married couple) into a Trust during your lifetime, or $2 million (or $4 million for a married couple) upon death, without incurring additional taxes.

For those individuals or couples seeking to maximize the ultimate value of their Generation-Skipping Trusts beyond the limits established by Congress, the maximum amount of lifetime transfers should be made. Such amounts will be offset against the $2 million exemption from the estate tax available at death to each individual. Once the trust is funded, all of the future appreciation of the Trust escapes both the GST tax, as well as estate taxes.

The key is to transfer assets into the Generation-Skipping Trust during your lifetime, and have the Trust assets increase in value free of estate tax and the GST tax. In planning for the investment of the assets inside the Trust, careful attention must also be paid to the income tax consequences.

A life insurance policy can be an excellent funding mechanism inside the Trust. From a tax and investment standpoint the use of life insurance policies with guaranteed death benefits can make a lot of sense. It also provides an emotional benefit by reducing worries about risks of the financial markets.

TAX BENEFITS

There are only two investment vehicles that escape income taxes under the current tax laws - - tax-exempt bonds and life insurance. The purchase of a life insurance policy with a guaranteed death benefit inside a Generation-Skipping Trust allows a person to effectively multiply the value of the Trust many times over without incurring any stock market risk or income tax liabilities during the accumulation phase or upon death.

In addition, because most Generation-Skipping Trusts are structured to provide for the younger generation upon the death of the older generation, the life insurance strategy can maximize the value of the Trust at the most appropriate time.

INVESTMENT BENEFITS

A life insurance policy should be analyzed in the same manner as any other investment, by focusing on the return on the invested premiums. Obviously, this would be a relatively simple calculation if you knew how long you would live and how the policy will perform. However, it is possible, and appropriate, to review the projected returns at life expectancy and beyond such time in order to review the investment merits of using a life insurance strategy.

In fact, we can compare the projected return on a life insurance policy versus investing the trust assets in tax-exempt bonds and calculate the point at which the bonds would be a better investment vehicle. This analysis typically demonstrates that life insurance makes much greater sense from an investment perspective as compared to tax-exempt bonds even if the insured lives well beyond life expectancy. Thus, unless the Trust is designed to provide cash flow, a life insurance strategy may make more sense from an investment perspective.

EXAMPLE 11

LIFE INSURANCE INVESTMENT ANALYSIS

Assume Mr. and Mrs. Smythe are both age 70 and are in excellent health. They decide to transfer their combined $2 million lifetime allowances to a Generation-Skipping Trust to be used to purchase a single premium life insurance policy with a guaranteed death benefit of almost $9.5 million.

If the trustee had used the $2 million to purchase tax-exempt bonds with a 4% yield, the last to die of either Mr. or Mrs. Smythe would have to live another 40 years before the $2 million would be worth the same amount guaranteed by the life insurance strategy.

EMOTIONAL BENEFITS

The use of life insurance policies providing guaranteed death benefits also adds the important component of certainty to a Generation-Skipping Trust. Once one of these life insurance policies has been purchased, there is an assurance that there will be a specified amount that will ultimately be paid to the Trust free of taxes. This can, in turn, provide the person who established the Trust with the emotional comfort to use all of their other assets, as needed, or to engage in charitable planning, without being worried about providing their children with a diminished inheritance.

EFFECTIVE INSURANCE PLANNING

Any decision regarding the use of life insurance should be based on four major components - - quality of the company issuing the policy, quality of contract, underwriting and pricing. Let's explore each of these issues.

QUALITY OF COMPANY

First and foremost, you should only consider a contract that is offered by a top-tier carrier. In this regard, you can utilize the Comdex index, which assigns insurance companies a score of 1 to 100, based on the independent reviews of the various rating authorities including A. M. Best, Standard & Poor's, Moody's, Duff & Phelps, Weiss and Fitch. You should choose only companies with high ratings (at least 90), although companies rated in the mid-90's and higher are recommended.

QUALITY OF CONTRACT

The next issue is to select the most appropriate contract, based on the particular situation. This can often be difficult, because there are many different types of insurance policies in the marketplace, including term insurance, whole life, universal life, and various combinations of these. Each type is described below.

TERM INSURANCE

Term insurance is the right choice when a person has a specific need for a limited period of time, after which the need for the coverage expires. During the "need" period, premiums typically remain fixed for a set period of time, typically 10 to 20 years. Term premiums increase with age.

Term insurance is extremely profitable for the insurance companies, as they tend to insure people who are in good health, and most people outlive the period when the coverage remains affordable, and later drop the coverage when the price multiplies. In most cases, term insurance is inappropriate for permanent issues, such as estate and generation-skipping planning matters.

WHOLE LIFE INSURANCE

With a whole life policy, a fixed premium is required to guarantee the death benefit. While premiums are typically paid for a limited number of years, the actual number of premiums that must be paid is subject to the dividends declared by the insurance company, or a fixed interest rate.

Traditionally, whole life insurance was commonly used for permanent insurance planning matters. It was very popular for many years, as it had been the only type of policy that offered lifetime guarantees. However, due to the evolution of the insurance industry and increased competition, several top-tier insurance providers have developed less expensive universal life insurance policies with lifetime guarantees, causing many insurance companies to no longer offer whole life insurance policies.

UNIVERSAL LIFE INSURANCE

The most popular type of permanent insurance policy in today's estate planning marketplace is universal life. It is useful in solving a number of estate planning problems.

There are two types of universal life insurance policies - - guaranteed contracts and non-guaranteed contracts. With a guaranteed contract, you pay a fixed premium in exchange for a stated death benefit that remains guaranteed for your lifetime without contractual risk, provided that premiums are paid on a timely basis. This type of policy, which was developed about six years ago, has become extremely popular and is beneficial from a tax, investment and emotional perspective.

With a non-guaranteed contract, the policy owner assumes some of the risk that would typically be assumed by the insurance company. In exchange for assuming this risk, the policy owner is typically compensated, either with reduced premium commitments or increased death benefits.

Before purchasing a non-guaranteed contract, it is important to quantify the level of risk to make sure that it is reasonable. In addition, these policies should be compared to guaranteed contracts in order to determine whether the level of compensation is sufficient for the risk that is being assumed.

UNDERWRITING

In terms of underwriting, insurance companies base their pricing on "risk" rather than "health." While a person may be in excellent health, they may have certain risk issues that result in the insurance company imposing additional charges or refusing to issue a policy. On the other hand, persons assuming that certain ailments may make them uninsurable, are often pleasantly surprised by the actual pricing, as insurance companies have become more competitive with their underwriting decisions in recent years.

In addition to medical underwriting matters, the ability to obtain insurance coverage is dependent on financial underwriting. In this regard, an insurance company will limit the amount of coverage that it is willing to offer to an amount that is justified from an economic perspective.

This means that the amount of coverage will typically be limited to the projected need, or loss, that the insurance is designed to cover. It is important to understand both of these concepts.

For these reasons, it is recommended that you use the services of an experienced agent who is aware of your medical risks at the time of underwriting, and has the expertise to effectively negotiate with a variety of top-tier providers. By submitting applications to several insurance providers, the insurance companies must compete for your business, increasing the opportunity to acquire optimal pricing.

PRICING

Once you have identified the strongest companies and have decided on the most appropriate contract, it is important to obtain the most attractive policy from a pricing perspective. This means obtaining the maximum possible insurance for your dollar. The insurance industry is very competitive, and you should insist that your agent negotiate for the most attractive underwriting offer.

The cost of an insurance policy is based on two factors - - the type of contract that is being considered, and the underwriting or pricing of the policy. In terms of the type of policy, a single person will usually consider a policy that insures himself or herself, but a married couple has increased flexibility by utilizing individual coverage or a survivorship (or "second-to-die") policy that insures both husband and wife, and pays at the survivor's death.

With a survivorship contract, the insurance company is insuring two lives and does not pay until the second death, resulting in reduced risk and, accordingly, substantially lower pricing compared to individual coverage. These policies are often used inside a Generation-

Skipping Trust as the smaller premiums allow the trustee to purchase policies with larger death benefits when compared to individual policies.

TRADITIONAL INSURANCE PLANNING

As illustrated in Chapter Five, the combination of annual exclusion and/or lifetime gifting and insurance planning provides an individual or a married couple with the opportunity to leverage the ultimate value of the Generation-Skipping Trust well beyond those limits that would apply if the Trust were funded at death. In these cases, the trustee has the opportunity to use Trust assets to purchase a life insurance policy by paying premiums in one lump-sum, or on an annual premium basis.

COMBINING INVESTMENTS AND INSURANCE

While applying all of the Trust assets towards the funding of life insurance can be very attractive, many investors prefer to use traditional investments as well as a means of keeping the Trust partially liquid. In those situations, it makes sense to dedicate a reasonable portion of the Trust assets towards the funding of an annual premium life insurance policy with a guaranteed death benefit.

The use of the life insurance, coupled with additional traditional investments, is an effective way to diversify the Trust assets and add a degree of certainty to the ultimate value of the Trust. In addition, as long as the Trust assets continue to increase at a reasonable level, the liquidity should remain relatively constant.

EXAMPLE 12
COMBINING LIFE INSURANCE & INVESTMENTS

Mr. and Mrs. Smythe are both age 70 and in excellent health. They are fortunate in that their parents established a Generation-Skipping Trust many years ago. The Smythe's are entitled to the trust income during their lifetimes, and upon their death, the Trust continues for the benefit of their three children.

Since the Smythe's have no need for the trust income, they have allowed it to grow over the years. However, while the Trust was worth $5 million three years ago, it has declined to $4 million since that time. As a means of increasing the ultimate value of the Trust and providing certainty to their children, the trustee dedicates 2% of the Trust value, or $80,000, each year to fund a second-to-die life insurance policy with a guaranteed death benefit of $5.5 million.

The funding of the life insurance policy provides the Smythe's with an attractive investment that immediately enhances the value of the Trust, and assures them that the Trust will always be sizeable irrespective of the performance of the other Trust assets.

ADVANCED PLANNING TECHNIQUES

In the investment marketplace, there are many times when we hear about particular techniques that sound too good to be true. Typically, they truly are "too good to be true." It is critical that you determine the risks and rewards of each strategy prior to making any purchase. This can only be accomplished by selecting qualified and experienced advisors who can communicate these complex issues in an understandable manner.

Three of the most common advanced planning strategies that are frequently utilized by wealthy families to expand their Generation-Skipping Trusts are explained below.

SPLIT DOLLAR LIFE INSURANCE

If assets are transferred into a Generation-Skipping Trust to fund a life insurance policy, the death benefit is limited to the amount that can be purchased with the gift. In order to purchase larger policies without triggering gift taxes, one can lend assets to the Trust. This is particularly attractive, as loans are not necessarily considered transfers for gift or generation-skipping tax purposes if structured properly.

A split-dollar arrangement is a way to fund the purchase of life insurance through a sharing of costs between the grantor, or their closely-held business, and the Generation-Skipping Trust. The gift component is calculated based on the equivalent cost of purchasing term insurance on the insured(s). Because this amount is typically much lower than the amount transferred, a much larger amount of assets can be transferred to the Trust without triggering gift tax consequences, allowing the Trust to purchase a much larger amount of coverage.

The income, gift and estate taxation of life insurance owned in conjunction with a split-dollar program is the subject of recently issued comprehensive Treasury regulations. Many aspects of the taxation and accounting treatment of split-dollar life insurance arrangements including, but not limited to, the timing, incidence and amount of taxation, are covered in the final regulations, and competent legal, tax and/or accounting advice should be sought, especially in respect of the effect of these regulations on existing split dollar plans.

PREMIUM-FINANCING

Another way to purchase life insurance in a Generation-Skipping Trust is by using premium financing. For those who are relatively illiquid, or who want to use leverage to increase the Trust's value, premium financing may be the answer. This concept has gained popularity as a means of funding life insurance without incurring gift taxes.

This technique is complex, and carries significant economic risks. Accordingly, a competent tax advisor should be engaged to work together with your insurance agent to implement this strategy.

PRIVATE PLACEMENT LIFE INSURANCE

As you are well aware, the growth of traditional investments is ultimately subject to income and, possibly, capital gains taxes, while the growth of life insurance contracts permanently avoids income taxes. In certain circumstances, a wealthy family can acquire a customized life insurance policy, known as a "private placement life insurance policy," to effectively avoid these income tax consequences.

Unlike retail life insurance policies, these contracts may allow a policy owner to design a contract at a reduced cost and acquire substantial income tax benefits, as well as the flexibility to change investment alternatives free of income tax consequences.

These policies have become popular in recent years as an alternative means of owning hedge fund investments and for those seeking to protect their assets from the risk of potential creditors.

CHAPTER 8

DISCOUNTING TECHNIQUES

The use of a Family Limited Partnership (FLP) or a Family Limited Liability Company (FLLC) has gained popularity in recent years as a means of transferring assets to younger generations in a tax-efficient manner. In addition, when used properly, these techniques can increase the likelihood that particular family assets will remain within the family unit and benefit family members for several generations irrespective of the estate tax considerations. Each of these techniques will be explored in this chapter.

THE FAMILY LIMITED PARTNERSHIP

A FLP is a partnership that exists among members of a family as a means of managing family assets and transferring ownership from one generation to the next. The FLP is usually comprised of two types of partners - - "general partners" who control the day-to-day operations of the partnership, and "limited partners" who have no voice in management.

THE FAMILY LIMITED LIABILITY COMPANY

A FLLC is an alternative form of asset ownership that is very similar to the FLP. An FLLC consists of "managers" that manage the company, and "members" that act as passive investors. Similar to the FLP, the older generation can be the managers, and transfer membership interests to the younger generation on a discounted basis.

ESTATE PLANNING CONTEXT

Before discussing these techniques, caution must again be advised. The Internal Revenue Service has traditionally paid close attention to these entities, and requires that there be substantial non-tax reasons for their use. Careful attention must also be paid to assure that all owners comply with all of the requirements and terms of the FLP or FLLC agreement.

A FLP or FLLC is frequently used when a family desires to transfer ownership of assets for estate and gift tax purposes while retaining the ability to exercise control. Typically, business or real estate assets are transferred from individual ownership into the FLP or FLLC. The senior generation usually retains general partnership or management interests, and transfers limited partnership or membership interests to the younger generations or, even better, to a Generation-Skipping Trust for the benefit of the younger generations.

The FLP and FLLC form of ownership offers two unique advantages that are unavailable with other techniques:

- the ownership of assets can be transferred from one generation to the next without relinquishing control over the management or enjoyment of the FLP or FLLC assets; and

- the value of the assets that are typically transferred (i.e., the limited partnership or membership interests) can be substantially discounted for gift and estate tax purposes.

BENEFIT OF VALUATION DISCOUNTS

In the context of estate planning, the opportunity to utilize valuation discounts enables the senior generation to effectively transfer assets to younger generations, through a gift or sale, at a substantially discounted value. There are two major reasons for discounting the value of limited ownership interests for gift tax purposes:

- the owner(s) of the limited partnership interests (or membership interests) have no voice in the management of the FLP (or FLLC), and they cannot compel distributions at any time; and

- the lack of marketability of the FLP or FLLC interests resulting from the restrictions on transfer set forth in the agreement and pursuant to state law.

71

Accordingly, the value of these interests for transfer tax purposes may be substantially less than their proportionate share of the value of the assets owned by the FLP or FLLC. Thus, these interests may be subject to "minority interest" and/or "marketability" discounts, which can significantly reduce the value of the property transferred to them, assuming that such discounts are supported by an appraisal of the units which are transferred.

In turn, when the limited partnership interests are later transferred to younger generations, the gift, estate and generation-skipping tax consequences are based on the discounted value of the limited partnership interests rather than the actual value of the underlying FLP or FLLC assets. By using these valuation discounts, the transferor of limited partnership interests is able to remove these assets from his or her taxable estate at a more rapid pace as compared to the transfer of other assets.

EXAMPLE 13
TRANSFER OF DISCOUNTED FLP/FLLC INTERESTS

Mr. and Mrs. Smythe are concerned about transferring the owner-ship of their real estate holdings, currently worth $10 million, to their children. Upon the advice of their tax attorney, Mr. and Mr. Smythe transfer their real estate interests into the Smythe Family Limited Partnership in exchange for a 1% general partnership inter-est and a 99% limited partnership interest.

Mr. and Mrs. Smythe subsequently obtain an appraisal of the partnership interests, and are informed that a valuation discount of 35% is applicable to the limited partnership interests. They immediately transfer a 30% limited partnership interest to a generation-skipping trust for the ultimate benefit of their three children and six grandchildren.

By utilizing the valuation discounts, the Smythe's are able to trans-fer almost 50% more assets by using the FLP structure as compared to an outright transfer of their real estate holdings. They can imme-diately transfer property with an underlying value of approximately $3 million (the 30% limited partnership interest) with their two $1 million gift tax exemptions combined.

Extreme caution is advised when using these techniques because they are a frequent target for the IRS and the subject of adverse judicial decisions. These strategies should only be used if recommended and implemented by a qualified tax attorney.

S CORPORATIONS

A person who owns stock in an "S" corporation may not be allowed to transfer the stock ownership to a FLP or FLLC. In this situation, similar tax benefits to those described above remain available through a different avenue.

In this case, the ownership of the corporation can be re-structured by issuing "voting" and "non-voting" stock. The non-voting stock would be entitled to similar valuation discounts due to the lack of control and marketability. The same technique can be used with a "C" corporation if the stockholder does not wish to establish a FLP or FLLC.

THE INTENTIONALLY DEFECTIVE TRUST

An excellent tax-efficient technique often used by high net worth families involves the sale of FLP or FLLC interests, or non-voting stock in an "S" corporation, to an Intentionally Defective Generation-Skipping Trust (IDGST).

An IDGST is an irrevocable trust that is structured so that it is effective for estate and gift tax purposes, but will not be recognized for income tax purposes. This seemingly confusing concept results in the avoidance of all income tax consequences resulting from the sale of assets to the trust, as it is viewed as a sale by the grantor to himself or herself.

The typical sequence consists of first establishing and funding a FLP or FLLC. Subsequently, the grantor creates a IDGST that will purchase the limited partnership or membership interests at a discounted value from the grantor in exchange for a promissory note.

Prior to purchasing the FLP or FLLC interests, the Trust is typically initially funded with assets equivalent to at least 10% of the value of the FLP or FLLC units that will be sold to the trust to demonstrate that the trust will be able to service the promissory note. This funding is a taxable gift, and is offset against the grantor's gift tax exemption(s).

Because the transaction is structured as a sale rather than a gift, the sale avoids all gift and generation-skipping taxes as long as the value of the note equals the value of the interests purchased. In addition, because the grantor is treated as the owner of the trust for income tax purposes, there are no income tax consequences, meaning that capital gains taxes are avoided and the interest payments on the promissory note escapes income taxes.

Upon the death of the grantor, the value of the promissory note will probably be included in the taxable estate of the grantor. However, the assets in the trust, the limited partnership or membership interests, plus all appreciation, will escape estate taxes.

EXAMPLE 14
THE INTENTIONALLY DEFECTIVE GST

Mr. and Mrs. Smythe transfer $2 million, using their lifetime gift tax exemptions to an IDGST. They subsequently transfer income-producing real estate assets worth $20 million to the Smythe FLP in exchange for a 1% general partnership interest and a 99% limited partnership interest. Mr. and Mrs. Smythe obtain an appraisal of the partnership interests, and are informed that a valuation discount of 35% is applicable to the limited partnership interests.

After a few months, they engage in a sale of their 99% limited partnership interests to the IDGST in exchange for a promissory note in the amount of $13 million. The note is structured so that the IDGST is only required to pay interest at a 5% rate (based on then-applicable IRS interest rates), with the outstanding balance payable in 20 years.

The annual interest on the note is easily paid by the assets in the IDGST, which also receives annual partnership distributions from the FLP of $1 million. After 20 years, the value of the real estate has increased from $20 million to $50 million, and the IDGST assets have increased to $10 million. The outstanding amount of the promissory note is re-paid to the Smythe's, and the value of the Trust escapes all estate tax and GST tax consequences.

In this case, the Smythe family has realized enormous estate tax savings. They were able to transfer the lion's share of their real estate holdings outside of their taxable estate at a discounted value, further reduced their taxable estate by paying income taxes on FLP distributions to the IDGST, and transferred all of the appreciation of the real estate to a Generation-Skipping Trust that will escape estate taxes for decades if not centuries.

EXAMPLE 15
THE IDGST & LIFE INSURANCE

The same facts used in Example 14 occur with one major difference. Rather than investing the excess Trust assets and partnership distributions in traditional investments, they dedicate $300,000 annually to fund the purchase of a second-to-die life insurance policy with a guaranteed death benefit of $20 million.

Upon death, the IDGST is supplemented by the value of the insurance proceeds, which escape income taxes, estate taxes and GST taxes. These assets are used to re-pay the outstanding amount on the promissory note, with the excess invested for the benefit of future generations of the Smythe family.

Again, this example demonstrates the benefits of the IDGST strategy which, when coupled with life insurance, becomes even more powerful as a means of establishing the foundation of a family's wealth for generations to come. However, as always, this type of transaction should only be undertaken with the advice of competent counsel.

CHAPTER 9

CASE STUDIES

One of the best ways to illustrate the benefits of generation-skipping planning is to create a handful of case studies that cover a wide variety of circumstances. Most importantly, while these examples may provide you with an idea that may be of interest to you, it is critical that your actions make sense in light of your priorities and do not create any financial or emotional stress. Once you are assured that you have the means and desire to undertake this planning, you should arrange a meeting with your trusted advisors to determine the most appropriate plan.

The following case studies reflect "real life" situations that I encounter on a daily basis, including:

- protective parents;

- parents of children who have asset protection needs;

- wealthy seniors unwilling to maximize their annual gifting;

- seniors seeking to provide for their grandchildren;

- parents wishing to provide for children of a prior marriage in an efficient manner;

- well-to-do couples approaching retirement;

- parents seeking to provide for charity as well as their family; and

- family business owners who wish to transfer ownership to their children.

I hope these examples help you understand how generation-skipping planning may benefit you and your family.

THE PROTECTIVE PARENTS

FAMILY PROFILE:

      SINGLE FEMALE, LATE 60's

      NET WORTH, $1.5 MILLION

      2 CHILDREN, 4 GRANDCHILDREN

PRIORITIES:

      MAINTAIN INCOME

      PROVIDE FOR FAMILY

      PROTECT ASSETS FOR CHILDREN

CURRENT ESTATE PLAN:

      OUTRIGHT TO TWO CHILDREN

This woman has several priorities - - to make sure she always has sufficient income, to transfer her assets to her children upon her death, hoping that her grandchildren will eventually benefit from her net worth, and to protect the assets from spouses and excessive spending.

The simple solution is to amend her will or living trust so that, upon her death, her assets pass to a Generation-Skipping Trust that will provide for her two children for their lifetimes, and pass to the grandchildren thereafter. The Trust will be crafted so that 5% of the Trust will be paid to each child annually, plus additional amounts for health, education, support or welfare, subject to the discretion of an independent trustee.

MY DAUGHTER, THE DOCTOR

FAMILY PROFILE:
    MARRIED COUPLE, MID 50's
    NET WORTH OF $1.8 MILLION
    1 DAUGHTER, A PHYSICIAN

PRIORITIES:
    MAINTAIN INCOME
    PROVIDE FOR SINGLE DAUGHTER

CURRENT ESTATE PLAN:
    ALL ASSETS OWNED JOINTLY
    PAYABLE TO DAUGHTER AT AGE 50

This couple has the luxury of pensions that provide them with sufficient income during their lives. They recognize that their daughter will eventually inherit a substantial amount of assets. They are particularly concerned that their daughter had stopped paying for malpractice insurance, and that she could be exposed to lawsuits. In addition, they are worried about their single daughter marrying someone who could take advantage of her wealth.

The solution is to amend their estate planning documents so that their assets would pass to a Generation-Skipping Trust rather than directly to their daughter upon their death. Even though the daughter will be named as trustee and will be entitled to income plus principal for health, education, maintenance or support, the assets will be protected from lawsuits and any future spouse.

WELL-TO-DO SENIORS

FAMILY PROFILE:
>MARRIED COUPLE, EARLY-TO-MID 70's
>NET WORTH, $6 MILLION
>3 DAUGHTERS, 5 GRANDCHILDREN

PRIORITIES:
>MAINTAIN INCOME
>PROVIDE FOR DAUGHTERS
>MINIMIZE ESTATE TAX EXPOSURE

CURRENT ESTATE PLAN:
>$4 MILLION EXEMPT
>OUTRIGHT TO 3 DAUGHTERS

The simple solution is to establish a Generation-Skipping Trust that will be the centerpiece of their estate plan, and to update their legal documents to capture any remaining generation-skipping exemption at their deaths.

Although this couple is unwilling to maximize their annual gifts ($24,000 x 8 beneficiaries), they may be willing to transfer a smaller amount (e.g., $30,000) to reduce their estate tax exposure. The $30,000 would be transferred to the Trust every year to fund a second-to-die life insurance policy with a guaranteed death benefit of $1.5 million. Upon the survivor's death, their assets would flow, to the extent of their remaining generation-skipping exemptions, into the Generation-Skipping Trust, with any excess passing directly to their daughters.

WEALTHY SENIOR

FAMILY PROFILE:
 SINGLE FEMALE, EARLY 70's
 NET WORTH, $10 MILLION
 2 CHILDREN, 4 GRANDCHILDREN

PRIORITIES:
 WILLING TO MAXIMIZE GIFTS
 PROVIDE FOR GRANDCHILDREN & CHARITY
 MINIMIZE ESTATE TAX EXPOSURE

CURRENT ESTATE PLAN:
 FIRST $2 MILLION EXEMPT
 OUTRIGHT TO GRANDCHILDREN

Due to poor advice, her will was designed so that all of her assets would pass in trust to her four grandchildren at her death, exposing her to more than $5.5 million of estate and GST tax.

The solution is to establish four separate Generation-Skipping Trusts for her grandchildren, initially funded with her $1 million gift tax exemption, and supplemented with annual gifts of $12,000. Each Trust will own a combination of growth stocks and a life insurance policy, helping to ensure that there will be plenty of assets available to benefit the grandchildren. Since each grandchild is assured to receive a substantial inheritance, she feels comfortable enough to leave her remaining assets to her alma mater to fund a scholarship for years to come.

SECOND MARRIAGE

FAMILY PROFILE:

    SECOND MARRIAGE, MALE, AGE 65

    NET WORTH, $12 MILLION

    2 CHILDREN FROM FIRST MARRIAGE

PRIORITIES:

    WILLING TO MAXIMIZE GIFTS

    PROVIDE FOR WIFE AND CHILDREN

    MINIMIZE ESTATE TAX EXPOSURE

CURRENT ESTATE PLAN:

    FIRST $4 MILLION EXEMPT

    DIVIDED AMONG 2 CHILDREN AND WIFE

After learning that his children would share approximately $5.5 million after $2.5 million of estate taxes were paid, he decides to establish a Generation-Skipping Trust for the benefit of his two children and, ultimately his three grandchildren. The Trust will be funded with his wife's $1 million gift tax exemption, and will be supplemented with annual exclusion gifts of $12,000 for ten years.

The Trust assets will be used to fund the purchase of an individual life insurance policy on his life with a guaranteed death benefit of $7.5 million. The Generation-Skipping Trust will be supplemented at his death with his remaining $2 million of generation-skipping exemption free of additional estate taxes, providing them with $9.5 million, and leaving his wife with the remaining investment assets of $9 million.

WELL-TO-DO YUPPIES

FAMILY PROFILE:
>   MARRIED COUPLE, LATE 40's
>   NET WORTH, $8 MILLION
>   3 SONS

PRIORITIES:
>   UNWILLING TO MAXIMIZE GIFTS
>   MINIMIZE ESTATE TAX EXPOSURE

CURRENT ESTATE PLAN:
>   ALL ASSETS OWNED JOINTLY
>   PAYABLE TO 3 SONS AT AGES 25, 30 & 35

To address their current estate tax exposure, the husband transfers ownership of the $2 million insurance policy to a Generation-Skipping Trust. Because the husband is the sole grantor, the wife is named as trustee with control and discretionary rights to income and principal, providing her with sufficient comfort to transfer the husband's $1 million gift tax exemption to the Trust, and make annual exclusion gifts of $12,000 on behalf of their children. This will remove the life insurance from their taxable estate, provided he lives at least three years after the transfer, saving almost $1 million of estate taxes.

CHARITABLE PLANNING

FAMILY PROFILE:
>MARRIED COUPLE, EARLY 60's
>NET WORTH, $25+ MILLION
>4 CHILDREN

PRIORITIES:
>WILLING TO MAXIMIZE GIFTS
>PROVIDE FOR CHILDREN & CHARITY
>MINIMIZE ESTATE TAX EXPOSURE

CURRENT ESTATE PLAN:
>FIRST $4 MILLION EXEMPT
>20% OUTRIGHT TO EACH CHILD & CHARITY

To reduce their current estate tax exposure of $7 million, and properly provide for charity, they decide to transfer their $2 million of lifetime gift tax exemptions, plus $50,000 annually, to a newly-established Generation-Skipping Trust that will purchase $20 million of second-to-die life insurance.

Because they have accomplished their objective of providing each child with $5 million through life insurance, the balance of their assets will pass after taxes, at the survivor's death, to a Charitable Foundation, satisfying their philanthropic desires, and eliminating all estate tax exposure. The Charitable Foundation provides them with the peace of mind that their assets will benefit a variety of organizations, depending on the rules established by them, and the directions of their children.

INCOME-PRODUCING REAL ESTATE

FAMILY PROFILE:
>SINGLE FEMALE WITH WEALTHY PARENTS
>NET WORTH, $2.5 MILLION
>1 DAUGHTER, 2 GRANDCHILDREN

PRIORITIES:
>RE-STRUCTURE PARENT'S PLANNING
>MINIMIZE FAMILY'S ESTATE TAX EXPOSURE

CURRENT ESTATE PLAN:
>FIRST $2 MILLION PROTECTED

The objective is to have her parents create a Generation-Skipping Trust to keep as many assets as possible from transferring into her estate and being subjected to estate tax on multiple occasions.

The solution is to create a Family Limited Partnership that will be the owner of the parent's most valuable asset, an apartment complex worth $10 million, and producing $1 million of annual cash flow. The limited partnership interests will be sold at a substantial discount to an IDGST, so the majority of the cash flow will be directed into the FLP and, ultimately, to the trust.

The net result is that their taxable estate will be reduced to the extent of the discount, the future growth of the property will occur outside, rather than inside their taxable estate, and the bulk of the cash flow will be re-directed out of their taxable estate.

CHAPTER 10

GENERAL QUESTIONNAIRE

In order to reduce legal costs, you should be prepared when meeting with your estate tax professionals. To assist you and your advisors, my attorney, David Pratt, and I have prepared a broad questionnaire that addresses the many issues that must be considered in crafting your "Sequoia Trust™" agreement. This should serve as an excellent starting point in your discussions with your personal tax advisor who, with your active involvement, will be given the role of crafting a document that could last hundreds of years.

HUSBAND'S FULL NAME   _____

DATE OF BIRTH   _____

SOCIAL SECURITY NUMBER   _____

HEALTH CONDITIONS   _____

WIFE'S FULL NAME   _____

DATE OF BIRTH   _____

SOCIAL SECURITY NUMBER   _____

HEALTH CONDITIONS   _____

HOME ADDRESS _____

_____

_____

E-MAIL ADDRESS _____

HOME TELEPHONE NUMBER _____

CELL PHONE NUMBER _____

SECONDARY ADDRESS _____

_____

_____

DATE OF MARRIAGE _____

ANY PRE-NUPTIAL AGREEMENT? _____

ANY OBLIGATIONS AT DEATH? _____

IF YES, PROVIDE DETAILS _____

_____

_____

ARE YOU U.S. CITIZENS?

HUSBAND _____

WIFE _____

IF NO, PROVIDE DETAILS _____

_____

_____

_____

HAVE YOU EVER FILED GIFT TAX RETURNS? _____

IF YES, PROVIDE DETAILS   _____

                                     _____

                                     _____

DO YOU EXPECT AN INHERITANCE?   _____

IF YES, PROVIDE DETAILS   _____

                                     _____

                                     _____

DO YOU HAVE AN ESTATE PLAN? _____

IF YES, PROVIDE DETAILS   _____

                                     _____

                                     _____

ARE YOU A TRUSTEE OF ANY TRUST? _____

ARE YOU A BENEFICIARY OF ANY TRUST? _____

IF YES, PROVIDE DETAILS _____

_____

_____

_____

DO YOU HAVE CREDITORS OR JUDGMENTS? _____

IF YES, PROVIDE DETAILS _____

_____

_____

_____

QUESTIONNAIRE FOR EACH CHILD

NAME _____

DATE OF BIRTH _____

PROFESSION _____

ADDRESS _____

_____

HOME TELEPHONE _____

ANY PRIOR MARRIAGES? _____

SPOUSE'S NAME _____

DATE OF BIRTH _____

PROFESSION _____

ANY PRIOR MARRIAGES? _____

GRANDCHILDREN _____

_____

ESTIMATED NET WORTH _____

IS ASSET PROTECTION A CONCERN? _____

ANY ADDITIONAL DETAILS/CONCERNS? _____

IF YES, PROVIDE DETAILS _____

_____

_____

	HUSBAND	WIFE	JOINT	TOTAL

REAL ESTATE:

RESIDENCES

PRIMARY   _____ _____ _____ _____

SECONDARY   _____ _____ _____ _____

OTHER   _____ _____ _____ _____

              _____ _____ _____ _____

INVESTMENT ACCOUNTS:

STOCKS   _____ _____ _____ _____

BONDS   _____ _____ _____ _____

MUTUAL FUNDS _____ _____ _____ _____

MONEY MARKETS _____ _____ _____ _____

OTHER INVESTMENTS:

EE OR HH BONDS _____ _____ _____ _____

PRIVATE STOCK _____ _____ _____ _____

	HUSBAND	WIFE	JOINT	TOTAL
CHECKING				
SAVINGS				
CD'S				
NOTES				
MORTGAGES				

IRA'S, PENSIONS:
<u>CUSTODIAN</u>

LIFE INSURANCE:
<u>COMPANY</u>

PROVIDE OWNER, BENEFICIARY & VALUES

	HUSBAND	WIFE	JOINT	TOTAL

ANNUITIES:
  COMPANY

_____	_____	_____	_____	_____
_____	_____	_____	_____	_____
_____	_____	_____	_____	_____

FOR EACH POLICY, PROVIDE BENEFICIARY

LIABILITIES:

HOME MORTGAGE _____ _____ _____ _____

MARGIN _____ _____ _____ _____

PERSONAL _____ _____ _____ _____

OTHER ASSETS:

CLUB
MEMBERSHIPS _____ _____ _____ _____

PARTNERSHIPS _____ _____ _____ _____

STOCK OPTIONS _____ _____ _____ _____

TRUSTS _____ _____ _____ _____

DEFERRED COMP _____ _____ _____ _____

PERSONAL PROPERTY:

JEWELRY _____ _____ _____ _____

ART _____ _____ _____ _____

CARS _____ _____ _____ _____

BOATS, AIRPLANES _____ _____ _____ _____

MISCELLANEOUS:

HAVE YOU MADE ANY PLEDGES TO CHARITY? _____

IF YES, PROVIDE DETAILS _____

_____

_____

ANY OUTSTANDING LOANS? _____

IF YES, PROVIDE DETAILS _____

_____

_____

ANY ACCOUNTS WITH OTHERS? _____

IF YES, PROVIDE DETAILS   _____

                             _____

                             _____

ANY UGMA OR ITF ACCOUNTS? _____

IF YES, PROVIDE DETAILS   _____

                             _____

                             _____

DO YOU OWN AN UMBRELLA POLICY? _____

DO YOU OWN LONG-TERM CARE INSURANCE? _____

TRUST QUESTIONNAIRE:

TRUSTEE(S):   _____

                             _____

INITIAL TRUSTEE(S)

_____

_____

SUCCESSOR TRUSTEE(S)

_____

_____

_____

BENEFICIARIES:

PRIMARY BENEFICIARIES

_____

_____

SUCCESSOR BENEFICIARIES _____

_____

PER STIRPES

_____

_____

PER CAPITA

_____

_____

TRUST PROTECTOR:

DO YOU WISH TO ESTABLISH A
MECHANISM TO
AMEND TRUST?   _____

NAME OF TRUST
PROTECTOR(S)   _____

                                      _____

                                      _____

INVESTMENT ADVISOR:

DO YOU WISH TO LEAVE
THIS DECISION TO TRUSTEE?   _____

DO YOU WISH TO DESIGNATE
AN INVESTMENT ADVISOR? _____

NAME OF INVESTMENT
ADVISOR(S)   _____

                                      _____

                                      _____

DISTRIBUTIONS:

DO YOU WISH TO PROVIDE
MANDATORY OR
DISCRETIONARY DISTRIBUTIONS? _____
DO YOU WISH TO PROVIDE
ACCESS TO PRINCIPAL
IF NEEDED? _____

DO YOU WISH TO PROVIDE
TRUSTEE WITH DISCRETION TO
PROVIDE ADDITIONAL ACCESS? _____

DO YOU WISH TO PROVIDE
BENEFICIARY WITH RIGHT
TO DEMAND ASSETS? _____

LIMITED POWERS OF APPOINTMENT:

DO YOU WISH TO ALLOW
A DESIGNATED PERSON
DICTATE TO WHOM ASSETS
WILL BE ULTIMATELY
DISTRIBUTED? _____

SHOULD THIS RIGHT BE
EXERCISABLE DURING
LIFETIME OR AT DEATH? _____

SHOULD POWER HOLDER
BE GIVEN THE RIGHT
TO CHANGE TERMS
OF THE TRUST?   _____

SHOULD CHARITY BE
DESIGNATED AS A POTENTIAL
BENEFICIARY?   _____

REMOVAL OF TRUSTEES:

DO YOU WISH TO
ESTABLISH A PROCESS
TO REMOVE TRUSTEE(S)?   _____

SHOULD THIS POWER BE
LIMITED OR RELATIVELY
BROAD?   _____

WHAT IS THE PROCESS
TO DETERMINE SUCCESSOR
TRUSTEE(S)?   _____

_____

_____

SITUS/DURATION OF TRUST:

WHERE WILL THE TRUST
RESIDE FOR TAX AND STATE
LAW PURPOSES?

_____

DO YOU WISH TO LIMIT
THE TRUST TO A DESIGNATED
PERIOD OF TIME?

_____

DO YOU WISH TO EXTEND
THE DURATION OF THE
TRUST AS LONG AS POSSIBLE?

_____

TERMINATION OF TRUST:

UNDER WHAT CIRCUMSTANCES
IS THE TRUST TO BE
TERMINATED?

_____

_____

_____

ABOUT THE AUTHOR

Chuck Banker is an Attorney, Certified Public Accountant, Chartered Financial Consultant and Chartered Life Underwriter.

After graduating from Brooklyn Law School in 1978, Chuck worked as a Tax Attorney for a Big Eight accounting firm for several years before joining one of the world's largest financial services institutions as a Corporate Tax Attorney. After several more years, Chuck relocated to their corporate headquarters in Princeton, New Jersey, where he held the position of Senior Tax Attorney, which carried the responsibility of being the spokesperson for the firm regarding U.S. tax matters.

Chuck has appeared on several television shows, and has been quoted by many major publications. He now resides in South Florida where he advises some of the firm's wealthiest families in trust, estate and insurance planning matters.

MY EDITOR

Jack Lee was the primary editor of this book. Jack is a Vice President and Senior Financial Advisor for a major international financial institution. He earned a BA and MA from the University of Maryland and served in the U. S. Navy as a Russian and Hebrew linguist. Jack is married and lives with his wife Cay in Brandon, Florida.

MY ATTORNEY

David Pratt is a partner in the Personal Planning department of Proskauer Rose LLP's Boca Raton office, where he counsels high net worth individuals and families with respect to estate, gift and tax reduction strategies, and trust and estate planning. He also represents beneficiaries and fiduciaries of estates and trusts regarding tax, and probate and trust law issues.

David is a Fellow of the American College of Trust and Estate Counsel and is Florida Board Certified in Taxation and Wills, Trusts and Estates. He is the Chair of the Fiduciary Income Tax Committee of the American Bar Association's Section of Taxation and Chair of the Long Range Planning Committee of the Florida Bar's Tax Section. He is also a past President of the Boca Raton and Palm Beach Tax Institutes. He is on the Board of Trustees and is the Chair of the Personal Advisory Committee of the Jewish Community Foundation of the Jewish Federation of South Palm Beach County.

David has been awarded an "AV" rating in Martindale-Hubbell, has published various articles on transfer tax and is a frequent lecturer, both to professionals and laypersons.

Additional copies of this book may be ordered at a price of $19.95, plus applicable sales taxes to Florida residents only. Multiple purchase discounts are available, applicable to orders of ten or more copies.

A sample of the Sequoia Trust™ is available to assist you and your attorney with the crafting of the most appropriate Trust for you and your family.

Please contact the author at www.chuckbanker.com
where you can also find additional information about
ordering a copy of the Sequoia Trust™.